5000 MUSICAL TERMS

5000 MUSICAL TERMS

A
COMPLETE DICTIONARY
OF
LATIN, GREEK, HEBREW, ITALIAN, FRENCH, GERMAN
SPANISH, ENGLISH,

AND SUCH OTHER
WORDS, PHRASES, ABBREVIATIONS, AND SIGNS

JOHN S. ADAMS

GYAN

Published by

Gyan Publishing House
5, Ansari Road
Daryaganj, New Delhi-110002
Phone: 011-47034999, 9811692060
E-mail: books@gyanbooks.com

Distribution Network
gyanbooks.com
India, USA, Canada, UK, Australia, France

ISBN : 978-81-212-9663-2 (PB)
First Published, 1851

2nd Impression 2023

Printed at: Gyan Press, Delhi.

5000 MUSICAL TERMS
Author: JOHN S. ADAMS

5000
MUSICAL TERMS:

A

COMPLETE DICTIONARY

OF

LATIN, GREEK, HEBREW, ITALIAN, FRENCH, GERMAN, SPANISH, ENGLISH,

AND SUCH OTHER

WORDS, PHRASES, ABBREVIATIONS, AND SIGNS

AS ARE TO BE FOUND IN THE WORKS OF

AUBER, BEETHOVEN, BERTINI, BURGMULLER, CARULLI, CRAMER, CZERNY, DONIZETTI, HAYDN, HANDEL, HERZ, HUNTEN, LABITZKY, LISTZ, MEYERBEER, MENDELSSOHN, MOZART, RINCK, SPOHR, THALBERG, WARREN, WEBER, AND OTHER EMINENT MUSICAL COMPOSERS.

THE WHOLE INCLUDING THE CELEBRATED DICTIONARIES OF DR. BUSBY, CZERNY, GRASSINEAU, AND HAMILTON.

ARRANGED, REVISED, AND CORRECTED

BY JOHN S. ADAMS.

TO WHICH IS ADDED A TREATISE ON PLAYING THE ORGAN OR PIANO-FORTE BY FIGURES, ETC.

THE TIME TABLE.

A 𝅝 is equal to 2 𝅗𝅥, or 4 𝅘𝅥, or 8 𝅘𝅥𝅮, or 16 𝅘𝅥𝅯, or 32 𝅘𝅥𝅰, or 64 𝅘𝅥𝅱.

A 𝅗𝅥 is equal to 2 𝅘𝅥, or 4 𝅘𝅥𝅮, or 8 𝅘𝅥𝅯, or 16 𝅘𝅥𝅰, or 32 𝅘𝅥𝅱.

A 𝅘𝅥 is equal to 2 𝅘𝅥𝅮, or 4 𝅘𝅥𝅯, or 8 𝅘𝅥𝅰, or 16 𝅘𝅥𝅱.

A 𝅘𝅥𝅮 is equal to 2 𝅘𝅥𝅯, or 4 𝅘𝅥𝅰, or 8 𝅘𝅥𝅱.

A 𝅘𝅥𝅯 is equal to 2 𝅘𝅥𝅰, or 4 𝅘𝅥𝅱.

A 𝅘𝅥𝅰 is equal to 2 𝅘𝅥𝅱.

DICTIONARY OF MUSICAL TERMS.

ABBREVIATIONS, denoting the language in which the terms are written, or from which they are derived: *F.*, French; *G.*, German; *Gk.*, Greek; *H.*, Hebrew; *I.*, Italian; *L.*, Latin; *S.*, Spanish; *Pl.*, Plural.

A.

A, the alphabetical name given to the sixth note of the scale of C in ascending.

A, (*I.*) to, for, by, at, &c.; as, *a tre*, for three.

AANES, a Greek term, applied to modes and tones.

ABACUS, an ancient instrument for dividing the intervals of an octave.

A BALLATA, (*I.*) in the manner of a ballad.

A BATTUTA, (*I.*) *by beating*, or in strict time, after an *ad libitum*.

ABBANDONASI, **ABBANDONATEMENTE**; **ABBANDONE**, *con*, **ABBANDONO**, *con*, (*I.*) with self-negation and abandonment. Despondingly; without restraint, making the time subordinate to the expression.

ABBASSIMENTO DI MANO, (*I.*) the falling of the hand in beating time.

ABBREVIATURE, (*I. Pl.*) contractions or abbreviations in musical notations.

ABBELLIMENTI, (*I.*) ornaments introduced to set off a plain melody.

A BENE PLACITO, (*I.*) at the pleasure of the performer.

ABKURZUNGEN, (*G.*) abbreviations.

ABSATZ, (*G.*) a section, or musical sentence.

ABSETZEN, } (*G.*) These words imply a style of performance
ABSTOSSEN, } similar to staccato.

ABWECHSELEND, (*G.*) alternating, as *mit Abwechselenden Manualen*, alternately from the great choir to the organ, &c.

ACADEMIE ROYALE DE MUSIQUE, (*F.*) the name given to the French Opera House.

A CAPELLA, (*I.*) in the church style.

A CAPRICCIO, (*I.*) at will, agreeable to our fancy.

ACATHISTUS, a hymn sung in the ancient Greek church in honor of the Virgin.

ACADEMIA MUSICALE, (*I.*) Musical academy. The first one was instituted at Vicenza, A. D. 1500.

ACADEMIE ROYALE, (*F.*) an academy of music, instituted at Paris, A. D. 1669.

ACADEMY, (MUSICAL,) musical meetings, held under a directing leader. The first of these in England took place A. D. 1710.

ACCADEMIA, (*I.*) a concert.

ACCAREZZEVOLE, in a persuasive and caressing manner.

ACCAREZZEVOLMENTE, same as *Accarezzevole*.

ACCELERANDO, (*I.*) with gradually increasing velocity of movement.

ACCELERATO, (*I.*) accelerated, increased in rapidity.

ACCENT, a slight stress placed upon a note to mark its place and relative importance in the bar.

ACCENTUARE, (*I.*) to accentuate; to perform with expressive accentuation.

ACCIACCATURA, (*I.*) a species of arpeggio.

ACCIDENTS, occasional sharps, flats, and naturals placed before notes in the course of a piece.

ACCIDENTAL CHORDS, those chords containing one or more notes foreign to its proper harmony.

ACCOLADE, (*F.*) the *brace* employed to connect two or more staves in piano-forte or harp music, and in scores.

ACCOMPAGNAMENTO, (*I.*) } an accompaniment.
ACCOMPAGNEMENT, (*F.*) }

ACCOMPAGNEMENS, (*F. Pl.*) accompaniments.

ACCOMPAGNATORE, (*I.*) } an accompanist.
ACCOMPAGNATEUR, (*F.*) }

ACCOMPANIMENT, a part added to a principal, by way of enhancing the effect of the composition. Accompaniments are sometimes *ad libitum*, that is, they may be dispensed with in the performance; and sometimes *obligato*, that is, indispensable to the proper effect of the whole.

ACCORD, (*F.*) a chord.

ACCORDARE, (*I.*) to tune.

ACCOMPANIMENT OBLIGATO, the accompaniment must be used.

ACCOMPANIMENT AD LIBITUM, use the accompaniment or not, at pleasure.

ACCOMPANIST, the person playing the accompaniment.

ACCOPIATE, the union of two parts.

A CEMBALO, or A CEMB., (*I.*) for the harpsichord.

ACCENTOR, an old term, signifying the performer who took the principal part in a duet, trio, &c.

ACCORD, TO, to agree in pitch and tone.

ACCORDANDO, (*I.*) tuning.

ACCORDATORE, (*I.*) }
ACCORDEUR, (*F.*) } a piano-forte tuner.

ACCORDO, (*I.*) a chord.

ACCORDATURA, (*I.*) the scale of notes, according to which the open strings of any instrument are tuned. Thus, C, G, D, A, form the accordatura of the tenor and of the violoncello; G, D, A, E, that of the violin; E, A, D, G, B, E, that of the guitar, &c.

ACCORDER, (*F.*) to tune an instrument.

ACCRESCIMENTO, (*I.*) an increase, or augmentation.

ACCRESCIUTO, (*I.*) superfluous; augmented in respect to intervals.

ACETABULUM, an instrument of the ancients.

ACHTELNOTE, (*G.*) a quaver.

A CHULA, a Portuguese dance, resembling the fandango.

A CINQUE, (*I.*) for five voices or instruments.

ACOUSTICS, from the Greek, denoting the science of sound.

ACTE DE CADENCE, (*F.*) a cadence.

ACUTE, high, shrill, as to pitch.

ADAGIO, (*I.*) very slow and expressive, admitting of much grace and embellishment.

ADAGIO ASSAI OR MOLTO, (*I.*) extremely slow and expressive.

ADAGIO CANTABILE E SOSTENUTO, (*I.*) a very slow movement, in a sustained or singing style.

ADAGIO PATETICO, (*I.*) in a slow time, and with plaintive expression.

ADAGISSIMO, (*I.*) excessively slow.

ADASIO, (*I.*) same as *Adagio*.

ADDITATO, (*I.*) fingered.

ADDITIONAL KEYS, an epithet applied to the keys of a piano-forte when they run above F in altissimo.

A DEMI VOIX, ——— JEU, } (*F.*) synonymous with *mezza voce:* see that term.

A DEUX TEMPS, (*F.*) two equal times or measure notes in a bar.

A DEUX, (*F.*) for two voices or instruments.

ADJUNCT NOTES, unaccented auxiliary notes.

AD LIBITUM, (*L.*) at will, or discretion. This expression implies that the time of some particular passage is left to the pleasure of the performer; or that he is at liberty to introduce whatever embellishments his fancy may suggest.

AD LONGUM, (*L.*) applied by the early reformers to compositions consisting of notes of equal duration, and those the longest in use.

AD OMNEM TONUM, (*L.*) from every note.

ADORNAMENTO, (*I.*) an ornament.

A DUE CORDE, instruments having two strings.

A DUE, (*I.*) for two voices or instruments.

A DUR, (*G.*) the key of A major.

ADQUISTA, applied by the Greeks to the sound added at the bottom of the scale in each of the modes.

ÆOLIAN PIANO-FORTE, a piano-forte so conjoined with the Æolian that the same set of keys serve for both, or for either, singly, at the pleasure of the performer.

ÆOLIDICON, a seraphine or melodeon.

ÆOLIAN HARP, an instrument the tones of which are caused by a vibration of the strings by the air.

ÆQUIVAGANS, (*L.*) a term used to signify that all the parts in the passage deviated from the natural order of the measure at the same time.

ÆQUISONANS, ÆQUISONANT, } of the same or like sound; a unison.

ÆSTHETICS, from the Greek; the doctrine of taste as applied to the fine arts; musical expression; causing sensations of beauty, sublimity, or pleasure.

AEUSSERSTE STIMMEN, (*G. Pl.*) the extreme parts.

AFFABILE, in manner kind and courteous.

AFFANNOSO, *con*, (*I.*) with mournful expression.

AFFETTUOSO, AFFETTUOSAMENTE, AFFETTO, *con*, (*I.*) with tenderness and pathos.

AFFLIZIONE, *con*, (*I.*) sorrowfully, with affliction.

AFFRETTANDO, AFFRETTATE, (*I.*) accelerating, hurrying the time.

A FOFA, a Portuguese dance resembling the fandango.

AGEVOLE, (*I.*) without labor, light, easy, agreeably.

AGITATO UN POCO, with slight agitation.

AGIA, used by the Greeks in characterizing modes or tones.

AGITATO ALLEGRO, a rapid and perturbed style of performance.

AGILITA, *con*, (*I.*) with lightness and agility.

AGITATO, AGITAZIONE, *con*, (*I.*) with agitation, anxiously.

AGNUS DEI, (*L.*) one of the principal movements of the mass.

AGOGE, employed by the Greeks as a name for one of the subdivisions of their Melopœia.

A GRAND CHŒUR, (*F.*) for the entire chorus.

A GRAND ORCHESTRE, (*F.*) for the entire or complete orchestra.

AGREMENS, (*F. Pl.*) embellishments.

A IN ALT, the A placed on the first upper added line.

A IN ALTISSIMO, an octave above A in Alt.

AIR VARIÉ, (*F.*) an air with variations.

AIR, (*F.*) an air or tune with or without words; as *Air Italien*, an Italian air, &c.

AIRS TENDRES, (*F.*) songs of an amatory description.

AIS, (*G.*) a sharp.

A LA MESURE, (*F.*) in time; synonymous with the Italian words *A tempo*.

ALBERTI BASS, a bass formed by taking the notes of chords in Arpeggios; this kind of bass is said to have been invented by one Dominico Alberti.

A LIVRE OUVERT, (*F.*) at sight; literally, at the opening of the book.

ALLIEVO, (*I.*) a pupil.

AL, ALL', ALLA, ALLO, (*I.*) to the, or in the style of.

AL FINE E POI CODA, at the close of the piece perform the Coda.

ALLA BREVE, (*I.*) this term is used to indicate a quick species of common time, formerly used in church music.

—— **CACCIA**, in the hunting style.

—— **CAPELLA**, (*I.*) in the sacred or church style.

—— **MADRE**, (*I.*) songs and hymns to the Virgin.

—— **MARCIA**, } (*I.*) in the military or march style.
—— **MILITAIRE**,

—— **MODERNA**, (*I.*) in the present or modern taste.

—— **POLACCA**, (*I.*) in the style of Polish dance-music.

—— **ROVERSCIO**, (*I.*) in contrary or reverse movement.

—— **RUSSE**, (*I.*) resembling Russian music.

—— **SICILIANA**, (*I.*) in the manner of Sicilian dance-music.

—— **SCOZZESE**, (*I.*) in the Scottish style.

—— **STRETTA**, (*I.*) increasing the time; accelerating the degree of movement.

—— **TEDESCA**, (*I.* in the German style.

—— **TURCA**, (*I.*) in the Turkish style.

—— **VENEZIANA**, (*I.*) in the style of Venetian music.

—— **ZOPPA**, in a constrained and limping style.

ALL' ANTICA, (*I.*) in the ancient style.

—— **ESPAGNUOLA**, in the Spanish style.

—— **INGLESE**, in the English style.

—— **ITALIANA**, in the Italian style.

—— **IMPROVISO**, (*I.*) suddenly.

—— **IMPROVISTA**, (*I.*) without previous study; unpremeditatedly.

—— **OTTAVA**, (*I.*) *in the octave.* This expression frequently occurs in scores, for the purpose of indicating that one part must play in the octave above or below another.

—— **UNISONO**, (*I.*) in *unison;* or occasionally in octaves.

ALLEGRAMENTE, (*I.*) with quickness.

ALLEGRETTO, (*I.*) somewhat cheerful, but not so quick as *Allegro.*

ALLEGRETTO SCHERZANDO, (*I.*) moderately playful and vivacious.

ALLEGREZZA, (*I.*) joy; as, *con allegrezza*, joyfully, animatedly.

ALLEGRISSIMO, (*I.*) extremely quick and lively.

ALLEGRO, (*I.*) quick, lively. A term implying a rapid and vivacious movement, but which is frequently modified by the addition of other words; as,

——— AGITATO, quick, with anxiety and agitation.

——— ASSAI, very quick.

——— COMODO, with a convenient degree of quickness.

——— CON BRIO, quick, with brilliancy.

——— CON FUOCO, quick, with fire.

——— CON MOTO, quick, with more than the usual degree of movement.

——— CON SPIRITO, quick, with spirit.

——— DI BRAVURA, quick, dashing and brilliant.

——— FURIOSO, quick, with fury.

——— MA GRAZIOSO, quick, but gracefully.

——— MA NON TROPPO, } quick, but not to excess.
——— MA NON PRESTO, }

——— DI MOLTO, exceedingly quick.

——— MOLTO, or DI MOLTO, extremely quick.

——— VELOCE, quick to absolute rapidity.

——— VIVACE, with vivacity.

——— VIVO, with great life and energy.

ALLEMANDE, (*F.*) a slow dance in common time of four crotchets in each measure.

ALLEGRI DI BRAVURA, brilliant and effective compositions.

ALLELUJAH, an ascription of praise.

ALLENTANDO, decreasing the time.

ALLONGER, (*F.*) to develop; to lengthen. This term sometimes occurs in violin music; as *allongez l'archet*, give development to the bow; lengthen the strokes of the bow.

ALMA REDEMPTORIS, (*L.*) a hymn to the Virgin.

AL LOCO, (*I.*) terms which refer us to some previous place in the piece.

AL RIGORE DI TEMPO, (*I.*) in strict time.

AL ROVERSCIO, (*I.*) by reverse or contrary motion.

AL SEGNO, } signifies that the performer must return
AL SEG. (abb.) or 𝄋 } to a similar character in the course of

the movement, and play from that place to the word *fine*, or the mark 𝄐 over a double bar.

ALMAIN, an air in common time.

ALT, a term applied to those notes which lie between F on the fifth line in the treble stave, and G on the fourth ledger line above.

ALT-GEIGE, } (*G.*) the tenor violin.
—— VIOLE, }

ALT-SCHLUSSEL, } (*G.*) the C clef on the third line.
—— ZEICHEN, }

ALTA, (*I.*) *higher;* for example, *ottava alta* means that we are to play an octave higher than the notes are written.

ALTERATIO, (*L.*) a term formerly applied to the doubling the value of a note.

ALTERATO, (*I.*) } augmented, with respect to intervals.
ALTERÉ, (*F.*) }

ALTERNAMENTE, each part to be performed alternately.

ALTITONANS, (*L.*) high sounding.

ALTERNATIVEMENTO, to sing the parts of two songs alternately.

ALTERNATIVO, (*I.*) alternating; proceeding alternately from one movement to another.

ALTISSIMO, (*I.*) extremely high as to pitch.

ALTISTA, (*I.*) } one who has an *alto* or *counter-tenor* voice.
ALTISTE, (*F.*) }

ALTO, (*I.*) in vocal music, indicates the counter-tenor, or highest male voice. It also indicates the part for the tenor in instrumental music.

—— CLEF, the C clef on the third line of the stave.

—— CONCERTANTE, the tenor of the little chorus which continues throughout the piece.

—— PRIMO, the highest alto.

—— RIPIENO, the tenor of the great cnorus which is performed at some particular place in a composition.

—— SECUNDO, the lowest alto.

—— TENORE, the highest tenor.

ALTRA, } (*I.*) other.
ALTRO, }

ALTRI, (*I. Pl.*) others.

ALTUS, the upper or counter tenor.

ALZAMENTO DI MANO, (*I.*) the elevation of the hand in beating time.

AMABILE, } (*I.*) amiably.
AMABILITA, *con*, }

AMAREZZA, *con*, (*I.*) with bitterness and affliction.

AMATEUR, (*F.*) a non-professional lover of music.

AMBITUS, a word once used to signify the distance between the highest and lowest notes.

AMBO, or AMBON, the desk at which the canons were sung in the early ages.

AMBROSIAN CHANT, the chant introduced by St. Ambrose into the church at Milan, in the fourth century.

AMBUBAJE. This, among the ancient Greeks, was the name of a society of strolling flute-players.

AME, (*F.*) the sound-post of a violin, tenor, &c.

A MEZZA VOCE, (*I.*) in a subdued tone.

——— ARIA, a melody of moderate tone; also, a style partly recitative.

AMEN, from the Hebrew, signifying *so be it*, *truly*, or *verily*.

A MOLL, (*G.*) the key of A minor.

A MORISCO, in the style of the Moorish or Morris dance.

AMOREVOLMENTE, (*I.*) with extreme affection.

AMOROSAMENTE, (*I.*) in a tender and affectionate manner.

AMORE, *con*, } (*I.*) adverbs, signifying a soft, gentle, and tender
AMOREVOLE, } style of performance.

AMOROSO, (*I.*) a word from which the performer learns that the movement to which it is prefixed should be performed in a soft and tender style.

AMPHIBRACH, a musical foot, accented thus: ⏑ — ⏑

AMPHIMACER, a musical foot, accented thus: — ⏑ —

ANACAMPTIC, from the Greek; the name to sounds produced by reflection, as in echoes.

ANACAMPTOS, used by the Greeks to denote a course of retrograde or reflected notes.

ANANES, a word applied by the ancient Greek church to their modes or tones.

ANALYSE, (*F.*) an analysis.

ANACREONTIC, in the drinking or Bacchanalian style.

ANAPEST, a musical foot, accented thus, ⏑ ⏑ —.

ANAPHORA. This term formerly signified the immediate repetition of a passage.

ANCORA, (*I.*) once more; repeat again.

ANCHE, (*F.*) the reed or mouthpiece of the clarinet, oboe, or of the various organ pipes which form the reed stops.

ANCILLIA, sacred shields, on which the ancient Greeks beat the time of their music.

ANCIA, (*I.*) the reed of the oboe, bassoon, &c.

ANDAMENTO, (*I.*) an accessory idea which the composer introduces in a fugue to relieve the subject and its answers, and to produce variety.

ANDANTE, (*I.*) a slow and distinct movement.

——— AFFETTUOSO, slow, and with much pathos.

——— CANTABILE, slow, and in a singing style.

——— CON MOTO, slow, and with emotion.

——— GRAZIOSO, slow, and gracefully.

——— MAESTOSO, slow, and with majesty.

——— NON TROPPO, slow, but not in excess.

——— PASTORALE, slow, but in a simple and pastoral style.

ANDANTINO, (*I.*) a little slower than *andante*.

ANEANES, Grecian modes and tones.

ANFANSGRÜNDE, (*G.*) the elements or principles.

ANFANGS RITORNELL, (*G.*) an introductory symphony to an air, &c.

ANGLAISE, (*F.*) a tune adapted for a country dance, in the English style.

ANGOSCIAMENTO, *con*, (*I.*) with anxiety, apprehensively.

ANHALTENDE CADENZ, (*G.*) a pedal note or organ point.

ANHANG, (*G.*) an adjunctive member to a musical sentence; a sort of coda.

ANIMA, *con*,
ANIMATO,
ANIMOSO, } (*I.*) with animation; in a spirited manner.

ANIMA DI MUSICA, animated music; to perform with full power and feeling.

ANLAGE, (*G.*) the plan or outline of a composition.

ANLEITUNG, (*G.*) an introduction. This term often occurs in the titles to German publications.

ANONER, (*F.*) to perform in a hesitating manner.

ANOMALIES, false scales or intervals, which exist in keyed instruments.

ANSATZ, (*G.*) the mouthpiece of a wind instrument.

ANSCHLAG, (*G.*) the percussion of a discord.

ANSPRACHE, (*G.*) intonation.

ANTECEDENT, the subject of a fugue, or of a point of imitation.

ANTHEM, a composition in the sacred style, the words of which are generally selected from the Psalms.

ANTIBACCHIUS, a musical foot, composed of two long notes and a short one.

ANTICIPATION, } a taking of a note or chord previous to
ANTICIPAZIONE, (*I.*) } its natural and expected place.

ANTICO, *all'* (*I.*) in the ancient style.

ANTICIPATING GRACE, an embellishing note which forestalls the succeeding note.

ANTIPHONE, responses made by one part of the choir to another, or by the congregation to the priest, in the Roman Catholic divine service.

ANTIPHONARIUM, a volume containing the responses made by one side of the choir to the chants of the other.

ANTIPHONS, dialogues on sacred subjects, chanted by the choirs of the early Christian church.

ANTIPHONY, portions of Scripture chanted or sung at religious festivals.

A PARTE EQUALE, a term used to designate two or more performers who sustain an equally difficult and important part.

APERTO, (*I.*) open; an adjective sometimes used to indicate the employment of the damper pedal.

APICNI, a term applied to those sounds which are distant one or more octaves, and yet concordant.

A PIACERE, } (*I.*) at the pleasure of the performer. See
A PIACIMENTO, } *Ad libitum.*

A PLOMB, (*F.*) with exactitude as to time.

APOTOME, the remaining part of an entire tone, after a greater semitone has been taken from it.

A POCO PIU LENTO, (*I.*) a little slower.

———— **MOSSO,** (*I.*) a little quicker.

APPRISE, a sign placed to direct the eye from the last note of a staff to the first of the succeeding one.

APPASSIONATO,
APPASSIONAMENTO,
APPASSIONATAMENTE, } (*I.*) with intensity and depth of feeling.

APPEAU, those tones which resemble the warbling of birds.

APPLICATUR, (*G.*) a position or shift on the violin, violoncello, &c.

APPOGGIATURA, (*I.*) a note of embellishment, generally written in a small character.

APPOGGIATO, (*I.*) dwelt, leaned upon.

APYCNOS, applied to the diatonic genus, from its being plain and easy, free from minute divisions, and having great or specious intervals, in comparison with the chromatic and enharmonic.

A QUATRE MAINS, (*F.*)
A QUATRO MANI, (*I.*) } for four hands, or for two performers on one piano-forte.

A QUATRO, (*I.*) for four voices or instruments.

ARBITRIO, subject to the judgment of the performer.

ARCATO, (*I.*) to be played with the bow.

ARCHET, (*F.*) a violin, violoncello, or double bass bow.

ARCO, (*I.*) a bow; as, *col arco*, with the bow.

ARCHEGGIAMENTO, (*I.*) the management of the bow in playing the violin.

ARCHLUTE,
ARCHILUTH, (*F.*)
ARCILIUTO, (*I.*) } a stringed instrument resembling the theorbo, and by some considered synonymous with it.

ARCHI LEUTO, a very large and long lute.

ARDITO, (*I.*) boldly, energetically.

ARETINIAN SYLLABLES, the syllables *ut*, *re*, *mi*, *fa*, *sol*, *la*, used by Guido d'Arezzo for his system of hexachords.

ARIA, (*I.*) an air or song. There are several species of airs; as,

——— BUFFA, a comic air.

——— CONCERTATA, an air with elaborate orchestral accompaniments.

——— D'ABILITA, an air of difficult execution.

——— DI BRAVURA, an air requiring great volubility of execution.

——— DI CANTABILE, an air in a graceful, singing, and flowing style.

ARIE FUGATA, an air, the accompaniments to which are written in the fugue style.

—— PARLANTE, an air more declamatory than melodious.

—— TEDESCA, an air in the German style.

ARIE AGIUNTE, (*I. Pl.*) airs added to or introduced in any opera, on subsequent performances.

ARIETTA, } (*I.*) a short air or melody.
ARIETTINA, }

ARIETTA ALLA VENEZIANA, (*I.*) little airs in the style of the Venetian Barcarolles.

ARIOSO, (*I.*) in the style of an air; vocal, melodious.

ARIOSE CANTATE, (*I. Pl.*) a kind of speaking air, which, by introducing frequent changes of measure and manner, first served to draw the line between air and recitative.

ARMER LA CLEF, (*F.*) This expression relates to the placing of the sharps or flats requisite for the key of the piece immediately after the clef.

ARMONIA, (*I.*) harmony.

ARMONICA, (*I.*) a musical instrument, generally constructed of glass.

ARMONIOSO, (*I.*) with harmony.

ARMONICI, a musical instrument, the tones of which are produced from globular glasses.

ARMONICI, (*I.*) harmonic.

ARMONIOSAMENTE, (*I.*) harmoniously.

ARMONISTA, (*I.*) one who is acquainted with the doctrine of harmony.

ARPA, (*I.*) a harp.

—— DOPPIA, (*I.*) a double-actioned harp.

ARPEGGIANDO, ARPEGGIATO, ARPEGGIO, } (*I.*) This word implies that the notes of a chord must be played in quick succession, generally from the lowest note to the highest, in imitation of the harp.

ARRANGEMENT, that extension, or selection and disposal of the movements and parts of a composition, which fit and accommodate it to the powers of some instrument or instruments for which it was not originally designed.

ARS MUSICA, the art of music.

—— COMPONENTIS, (*I.*) the art of composing.

ARS CANENDI, (*L.*) the art of singing.

ARSIS and THESIS, the raising and depressing of the hand in beating time.

ARTICOLARE, (*I.*) to articulate distinctly each note.

ART DE L'ARCHET, (*F.*) the art of bowing.

ARTICULATO, (*I.*) to be enounced with distinct articulation.

ARTIST, (*I.*) } a virtuoso; a first-rate performer.
ARTISTE, (*F.*) }

AS, (*G.*) A flat; as,

— DUR, A flat major.

— MOLL, A flat minor.

ASCULÆ, a name applied by the ancients to those who professed to perform on the organ.

ASPERGES ME, (*L.*) the commencement of the mass in the Catholic service.

ASPREZZA, *con*, (*I.*) dryly, with coarseness or harshness.

ASSAI, (*I.*) very; as, *presto assai*, very quick.

ASSOLUTO, alone.

ASSAYING, a flourish on the instrument before the commencement of a piece, to determine whether it is in tune.

A SUO ARBITRIO, (*I.*) } *Ad libitum*, at will as to time, the choice
——— COMMODO, } of the degree of movement being left to the performer.

A TABLE SEC, (*F.*) a term relative to the practice of vocal exercises unaccompanied by an instrument.

A TEMPO, } (*I.*) in time. A term used to denote that, after
A TEM., (*abbrev.*) } some short relaxation in the time, the performer must return to the original degree of movement.

A TEMPO DI GAVOTTA, (*I.*) in the time of a gavot; moderately quick.

——— GIUSTO, (*I.*) in strict and equal time.

——— ORDINARIO, (*I.*) in an ordinary or moderate degree of movement.

——— DELL ALLEGRO, in the time allegro; a quick movement.

A TRE, or A 3, (*I.*) } for three voices or instruments.
A TROIS, (*F.*) }

ATTACCA, } (*I.*) implies that the performer must directly
——— SUBITO, } commence the following movement.

ATTACCATO SUBITO, (*I.*) to be commenced immediately.

ATTENDANT KEYS, the relative key; the key of the dominant and its relative, and of the subdominant and its relative.

ATTO, (*I.*) any act of an opera; as, *Atto primo, Atto secondo,* — act the first, act the second.

ATTORI, (*I. Pl. mas.*)
ATTRICE, (*I. Pl. fem.*) } the principal singers in an opera.

ATTO DI CADENZA, (*I.*) a disposition of the parts which indicates a cadence: as when, at the end of a strain, the bass rises a fourth or falls a fifth.

AUBADE, (*F.*) a morning concert given in the open air.

AUDACE, *con,* (*I.*) with boldness.

AUFHALTUNG, (*G.*) a suspension.

AUFLOSUNG, (*G.*) the resolution of a discord.

AUFSCHLAG, (*G.*) the unaccented part of a bar.

AUFSTRICH, (*G.*) an up-bow.

AUFTAKT, (*G.*) See *Aufschlag.*

AUGMENTATION. In counterpoint and fugue this term implies that a subject is imitated in notes of greater length.

AUGMENTED INTERVALS, those which are a semitone greater than the major or perfect intervals.

AUGMENTED, an epithet applied to such intervals as are more than major or perfect.

AULETES, from the Greek, signifying a flute-player.

A UNA CORDA. (*I.*) on one string.

AUS, (*G.*) from, out, of, occurs in German titles.

AUSARBEITUNG, (*G.*) the elaboration or last finish of a musical composition.

AUSDEHNUNG, (*G.*) extension, expansion.

AUSDRUCK, (*G.*) expression.

AUSFÜHRUNG, (*G.*) performance.

AUSHALTUNG, (*G.*) the sustaining a note.

AUSHALTUNGSZEICHEN, (*G.*) the character called a *pause.*

AUSWEICHUNG, (*G.*) modulation.

AUTENTICO, (*I.*) authentic.

AUTHENTIC, a name given to those church modes whose melody was confined within the limits of the tonic (or final) and its octave.

AUTOS SACRAMENTALES, (from the Greek,) theatrical representations which the Spaniards formerly made in their churches at public religious festivals.

AUTHENTIC CADENCE, a perfect or final cadence in any key.

AUXILIARY NOTES, a term applied to such notes as stand on the next degree of the stave above or below any principal note.

——— SCALES, scales of the relative keys belonging to any principal key.

AVE MARIA, (*L.*) a hymn to the Virgin.

AVENA, (*L.*) an oaten straw. This reed is supposed to have been the third kind of musical instrument used by the ancients, and succeeded that formed of the horns of quadrupeds. The first was formed of shells.

A VISTA, (*I.*) at sight; *a prima vista*, at sight.

AZIONE SACRA, (*I.*) a sacred drama.

B.

BACCHIA, a Kamschatdale dance in $\frac{2}{4}$ time.

BACCHIUS, a musical foot, consisting of one short and two long notes.

BACCIOCOLO, (*I.*) a musical instrument common in some parts of Tuscany.

BACHELOR OF MUSIC, the first musical degree taken at the English universities. Abbreviated, *Mus. Bac.*

BADINAGE, (*F.*) playfulness.

BAISSER, (*F.*) to lower or flatten in pitch.

BALKEN, (*G.*) the bass-bar of a violin, &c.

BALLAD, a short and familiar song.

BALLATA, BALLATETTA, } (*I.*) a ballad.

BALLET, (*F.*) BALLETTO, (*I.*) } a theatrical representation of some story or fable, by means of dance or metrical action, accompanied with music. In England, the second or concluding piece of the evening's entertainment at the Italian Opera House is generally a ballet.

BALLET-MASTER, the artist whose province it is to superintend the rehearsals and performance of the ballet; and who not unfrequently invents the fable and its details himself.

BALLI INGLESI, (*I. Pl.*) English country dances.

——— DELLA STIRIA, (*I. Pl.*) Styrian dances resembling waltzes.

——— UNGARESI, (*I. Pl.*) Hungarian dances in $\frac{2}{4}$ time, usually accented on the weak part of the bar.

BALLO, (*I.*) a dance, or dance tune.

BANDA, (*I.*) a band.

BANDORE, } an ancient stringed instrument of the lute species.
BANDORA, (*I.*) }

BAR, lines drawn across the stave to divide the music in small and equal portions of duration; each of these small portions in themselves is also called a *bar*.

BARCAROLLE, (*I.*) airs sung by the Venetian gondoliers, or boatmen, while following their avocations. These melodies possess a simple and artless beauty, equally delightful to the unpractised and to the most cultivated ear.

BARCARUOLA, the song of the Venetian gondoliers.

BARD, a poet and musician.

BARITONE CLEF, the F clef placed on the third line.

BARITON, (*F.*) } a male voice, intermediate, in respect to pitch,
BARITONE, } between the bass and the tenor voices. Tam-
BARITONO, (*I.*) } burini, Badicalle, and H. Phillips are fine examples of this species of voice.

BAROCCO, (*I.*) } terms applied to music having a confused har-
BAROQUE, (*F.*) } mony, an unnatural melody, and full of modulations and discords.

BARRÉ, (*F.*) a term used in playing the guitar. It implies that a temporary nut is to be formed by means of the fore finger of the left hand.

BARRE DE MESURE, (*F.*) a bar line.

——— REPETITION, (*F.*) a dotted double bar.

BAS-DESSUS, (*F.*) a mezzo-soprano or second treble voice.

BASS, or BASE, the lowest part in music.

BASSA, (*I.*) lower; as, *Ottava bassa*, play an octave lower than the notes are written.

BASSE, (*F.*) the bass part in general, instrumental or vocal.

——— CHIFFREE, (*F.*) a bass figured to indicate the chords or harmony.

——— CHANTANTE, (*F.*) the vocal bass.

BASSE CONTRAINTE, (*F.*) a ground bass.

—— – **FONDAMENTALE,** (*F.*) the fundamental bass, composed of only the roots of the chords which form the harmonic tissue.

—— **FIGUREE,** (*F.*) the figured bass.

BASSGEIGE, (*G.*) the violoncello.

BASSETTO, (*I.*) a diminutive term, implying the little bass.

BASSO, (*I.*) the bass part.

—— **BUFFO,** (*I.*) the first bass singer in a comic opera.

—— **CANTANTE,** (*I.*) the first bass singer in a serious opera

—— **CONCERTANTE,** the lighter or more delicate parts of a composition performed by the violoncello or bassoon.

—— **CONTINUO,** a bass that is figured, to indicate the harmony.

—— **COSTULTO,** (*I.*) ground or constrained bass.

—— **FIGURATO,** (*I.*) the figured bass.

—— **FONDAMENTALE,** (*I.*) the fundamental bass.

—— **NUMERATO,** (*I.*) the figured bass.

—— **OSTINATO,** (*I.*) a ground bass.

—— **PRIMO,** the first bass.

—— **RECITANTE,** bass of the small chorus.

—— **RIVOLTATO,** (*I.*) a term used to signify that bass which, instead of being the fundamental or lowest note of the chord to which it is applied, consists of the third or fifth of the fundamental note.

—— **RIPIENO,** (*I.*) in instrumental music, implies the bass part to the *tutti* passages.

—— **SECONDO,** the second bass.

BASS-COUNTER, or **CONTRA-BASS,** the under-bass. That part which, when there are two basses in a composition, is performed by the double basses.

—— **VIOL,** a stringed instrument in the form of a violin, but much larger. It has four strings and eight stops, which are subdivided into semi-stops, and is performed on with a bow.

BASSON, (*F.*) bassoon.

BASSOON, a wind instrument.

BASSOONIST, a performer on the bassoon.

BASSUS, an old Latin term for the fundamental sounds of a harmony.

BASS-SCHLÜSSEL, } (G.) the bass clef.
——ZEICHEN, }

BASTANTE, (I.) enough, sufficient.

BATON DE MESURE, (F.) the roll of paper or other material with which the conductor of an orchestra marks the time.

BATTEMENT, (F.) } that species of shake called a *beat*.
BATTIMENTO, (I.) }

BATTRE LA MESURE, (F.) to mark the time by beating with the hand or with a stick, &c., to beat time.

BATTUTA, (I.) time, the accented part of the bar.

BATTERE, the down beat.

BAU, (G.) the structure, speaking of musical instruments, &c.

B CANCELLATUM, (L.) a sharp, (♯.)

B DUR, (G.) the key of B flat major.

BEAT, one of the principal graces in music.

BEATING TIME, marking the divisions of the bar by means of the hand or foot.

BECARRE, (F.) a natural, (♮.)

BEC, (F.) } the mouthpiece of a clarinet.
BECCO, (I.) }

—— POLACCO, (I.) the name of a large species of bagpipe, used in some parts of Italy.

BECKEN, a Turkish musical instrument.

BEGEISTERUNG, (G.) exaltation, excitement, poetical enthusiasm.

BEGLEITENDE STIMMEN, (G. Pl.) the accompanying parts.

BEGLEITER, (G.) an accompanist.

BEGLEITUNG, (G.) an accompaniment.

BELL, a well-known pulsative metallic machine, ranked among musical instruments.

—— OF A TRUMPET, HORN, &c., the wide, lower opening from which the sound is emitted.

—— METRONOME, a metronome with the addition of a small bell which strikes at the commencement of each bar.

—— TONE, a tone of voice of a remarkably clear, musical flow.

—— HARP, a very old instrument, supposed to be the *lyra* or *cithara* of the ancients.

—— METALLO DI VOCE, bell-like brilliancy and fullness of voice.

BELLEZZA, *con,* (*I.*) with beauty of expression.

———— DELLA VOCE, a beautiful, melodious voice.

BELLICOZAMENTE, (*I.*) in a martial style.

BEMOLIZZARE, (*I.*) to depress the pitch of the natural notes by applying a flat to them.

BEMOLLE, (*I.*)
BEMOL, (*F.*) } flat; as, *Si bemolle,* B flat.

BEN,
BENE, } (*I.*) well; as,

BENEDICTUS, (*L.*) a movement belonging to a mass of Roman Catholic morning service.

BENE PLACITO, (*I.*) at will.

BEN MARCATO, (*I.*) well marked. This expression indicates that the passage must be executed in a clear, distinct, and strongly accented manner.

BEQUADO, (*I.*)
BEQUARRE, (*F.*) } a natural, (♮.)

BESCHREIBUNG, (*G.*) a description.

BEYSPEIL, (*G.*) an example.

BIANCA, (*I.*) a minim.

BICINIUM, (*L.*) a composition in two parts.

BINARY MEASURE, common time.

BINDUNG, (*G.*) syncopation.

BINDUNGSZEICHEN, (*G.*) a tie or bind.

B IN ALT, the third note in alt.

B IN ALTISSIMO, the third note in altissimo.

BIRN, (*G.*) that part of a clarinet and basset-horn into which the mouthpiece is inserted.

BIS, (*L.*) twice. A term which indicates that a certain passage, distinguished by a curve drawn over or under it, must be performed twice; this abbreviation saves writing the passage over again.

BISCHERO, (*I.*) a peg of a violin, violoncello, &c.

BISCROMA, (*I.*)
BISCROME, (*F.*) } a semiquaver.

BIS DIAPASON, a double octave.

BIS UNCA, the old name for a semiquaver.

BISINIA, a term used in piano music to denote that notes performed by one hand are repeated by the other.

BIZZARO, (*I.*) a term which denotes that the movement to which this is prefixed is written in an irregular and fantastic style.

BLANCHE, (*F.*) a minim.

BLASEBALGE, (*G.*) the bellows of an organ.

BLASINSTRUMENT, (*G.*) a wind instrument.

BLASMUSIK, (*G.*) music for wind instruments.

B MOLL, (*G.*) the key of B flat minor.

BOCAL, (*F.*)
BOCCHINO, (*I.*) } the mouthpiece of a horn, trombone, or serpent.

BODEN, (*G.*) the back of a violin, tenor, &c.

BOGEN, (*G.*) the bow.

BOGENFUHRUNG, (*G.*) the management of the bow.

BOGENINSTRUMENT, (*G.*) a bow instrument.

BOGENSTRICH, (*G.*) a stroke of the bow.

BOLERO, a Spanish dance with castanets.

BOMBARDE, (*F.*)
BOMBARDO, (*I.*) } an old wind instrument of the hautboy species.

BOMBYX, a Greek instrument, formed of reeds.

BORDONE, (*I.*)
BOURDON, (*F.*) } the double open diapason stop in an organ.

BOURREE, (*F.*) a lively dance, in common time, beginning with an odd crotchet.

BOUTADE, an impromptu ballet in a fanciful style.

BOW, a round stick having little projections at each end to hold the hairs, which form the effective part.

B QUADRATUM, (*L.*) a term applied by the older theorists to the character now called a natural.

BRANLE, (*F.*) an old dance.

BRATSCHE, (*G.*) the tenor violin.

BRAVO, BRAVA, BRAVI, (*I.*) an exclamation of approval used in Italian theatres. The first term is masculine, the second feminine, and the third plural.

BRAVURA, *con*, (*I.*) with vigor, with boldness.

BRACED POINTS, points having braces over them, showing that the notes over which they are placed are to be performed in a style between that of legato and staccato.

BRACES, curved or straight lines indicating that the notes which they connect are to be played or sung together.

BRACCIO, or BRAZZO, a term applied to certain instruments that are played with a bow, and held up to the neck by the left arm, as the violin.

BRIOSO, (*I.*) with brilliancy and spirit.

BRIDGE, that part of a stringed instrument over which the strings are drawn.

BRODERIES, an old term applied by the French to casual, unstudied ornaments in performance.

B ROTUNDUM, (*L.*) A flat, (♭.)

BRUSCAMENTE, (*I.*) abruptly, coarsely.

BUCCINA, a wind instrument used by ancient soldiers.

BUFFA, BUFFO, (*I.*) comic. An actor or singer who takes the light and humorous parts in the Italian comic opera. This epithet is also applied to the pieces themselves; as, *opera buffa*, a comic opera.

BUFFET ORGAN, a very small organ.

BUFFO CARICATO, singing in caricature.

BUON CANTATE, a well-informed vocalist.

——— GUSTO, a performance in the best style, by one whose taste is unexceptionable.

——— MANO, a performer having perfect command of the most brilliant and effective styles.

BURLANDO, (*I.*) in a jesting and playful manner.

BURLESCO, (*I.*) with extravagant and even burlesque humor.

BURLA, comical, with great humor.

BURDEN, that part of a song which is repeated at the end of every stanza.

BURLETTA, (*I.*) a light species of musical drama, somewhat in the nature of the English farce.

C.

CABALETTA, (*I.*) a simple melody, of a pleasing and attractive character.

CACCIA, *alla*, (*I.*) in the hunting style.

CACOPHONY, a discordant combination of sounds, forming no regular harmony.

CADENCE, (*F.*) a shake; also a cadence in harmony; as, *cadence parfaite*, a perfect cadence; *cadence rompue*, an interrupted cadence.

CADENCE, a close in melody or harmony. An ornamental and extemporaneous passage introduced at the close of a song or piece of music.

CADENCE INTERROMPUE, } (*F.*) an interrupted cadence.
——— **ROMPUE,** }

——— **IMPARFAITE,** (*F.*) an imperfect cadence.

——— **PARFAITE,** (*F.*) a perfect cadence.

CADENZA, (*I.*) a cadence, or close, at the termination of a song or other movement, introducing some fanciful and extemporaneous embellishment. In modern music the cadenza is generally written in small notes.

——— **D'INGANNO,** (*I.*) an interrupted cadence.

——— **SOSPESA,** a suspended cadence.

CÆSURA, (*L.*) the rhythmic termination of any passage consisting of more than one musical foot. The last accented note of a phrase, section, or period.

CALAMUS PASTORALIS, (one of the first instruments used,) a simple reed or cane.

CALANDO, (*I.*) gradually diminishing in tone and quickness, becoming softer and slower by degrees.

CALASCIONE, (*I.*) a species of guitar.

CALCANDO, (*I.*) pressing upon, hurrying the time.

CALMA, *con,* } (*I.*) with tranquillity and repose.
CALMATO, }

CALORE, *con,* } (*I.*) with much warmth and animation.
CALOROSO, }

CAMBIARE, (*I.*) to change.

CAMERA, (*I.*) the chamber; as, *musica di camera,* chamber music.

CAMINARDO, (*I.*) flowing, with gentle and easy progression.

CAMPANELLA, } (*I.*) a little bell.
CAMPANELLO, }

CAMPANELLINO, (*I.*) a very little bell.

CAN, Welsh for *song.*

CANARIE, (*F.*) } a jig in $\frac{3}{8}$ or $\frac{6}{8}$ time.
CANARIES, }

CANCRIZANS, retrograde movement.

CANON, a species of uninterrupted imitation.

CANONE, (*I.*) a canon, or catch for several voices or instruments.

CANONE AL SOSPIRO, (*I.*) a canon, the parts of which come in at the distance of a crotchet rest from each other.

——— APERTO, (*I.*) an open canon.

——— CHIUSO, (*I.*) a canon in which the solution must be discovered, sometimes an enigmatic canon.

CANTABILE, (*I.*) in a melodious, graceful, and singing style. The performance should be smooth, elegant, and replete with feeling.

CANTANDO, (*I.*) This word, placed over a piano-forte passage, indicates that the sounds must be blended softly into each other, as in singing.

CANTANTE, (*I.*) a part which is intended for the voice.

CANTARE, (*I.*) to sing.

——— A ORECCHIO, (*I.*) to sing by ear; that is, without a knowledge of musical notation.

——— A ARIA, (*I.*) to sing without confining one's self to the music written.

——— DI MANIERA, (*I.*) to sing with a profusion of embellishments, without taste or discernment.

CANTATA, (*I.*) a species of composition for one voice, consisting of an intermixture of air and recitative.

CANTATRICE, (*I.*) a female singer.

CANTATILLA, }
CANTATINA, } (*I.*) a short cantata.

CANTICA, (*L.*) }
CANTICI, (*I.*) } canticles, or devotional songs.

CANTICLE, a hymn, or divine song.

CANTICUM, (*L.*) a canticle, or divine song.

CANTILENA, (*I.*) the melody, air, or principal part in any composition, generally the highest vocal part.

CANTO, (*I.*) the highest vocal part in choral music.

——— FERMO, (*I.*) a chant or melody; as also any subject consisting of a few long, plain notes, given as a theme for counterpoint.

——— FIGURATO, (*I.*) a figured melody.

——— GREGORIANO, (*I.*) the Gregorian Chant.

——— PLANO, (*S.*) }
——— PIANO, (*I.*) } the plain song or chant.

——— PRIMO, (*I.*) the first treble.

CANTO RECITATIVE, the combination of an air and a recitative.

—— SECONDO, (*I.*) the second treble.

CANTOR, CANTORE, } (*I.*) a singer.

CANTORIS, a term used in cathedral music, to indicate the passages intended to be taken by those singers who are placed on that side of the building where the *cantor* or *precentor* sits; that is, on the left hand side on entering the choir from the nave.

CANTUS, (*L.*) a song, chant, or melody; as,

—— AMBROSIANUS, the melodies or chants introduced into the church by St. Ambrose.

—— MENSURABILIS, a measured melody.

—— FIRMUS, (*L.*) the plain song, or chant.

—— FIGURATUS, (*L.*) embellished or figurate melodies or chants.

—— GREGORIANUS, the chants collected by St. Gregory.

CANTADOURS, strolling singers.

CANTICÆ, short interludes.

CANTILENA SCOTICA, an old and favorite Scotch air.

CANTORATE, the office or residence of a cantor.

CANUN, a Turkish stringed instrument.

CANZONE, (*I.*) an air in two or three parts.

CANCHERIZANTE, (*I.*) This term denotes that the piece is played in a retrograde style, beginning at the end and going back to the commencement.

CANZONET, CANZONETTA, } (*I.*) a short canzone, or song.

CAOINAN, an Irish requiem.

CAPO, (*I.*) the head or beginning.

CAPOTASTO, (*I.*) the nut of the finger-board of a violin, violoncello, &c.

CAPRICCIO, (*I.*) a fanciful and irregular species of composition.

CAPRICCIOSO, A CAPRICCIO, (*I.*) in a fanciful, capricious style.

CAPRICCIETTO, (*I.*) a short capriccio.

CAPRICE, (*F.*) a capriccio.

CAPISCOLUS, the leader of a band or choir.

CAPO D' ASTRO, sometimes used instead of *capotasto*, to signify the principal bridge.

CAPISTRUM, from the Greek; a kind of muzzle used by the ancient trumpeters, so formed as to extend horizontally across the face, and embrace and confine the cheeks, to prevent their bursting with the violence with which they blew the instrument; an accident to which, without such precaution, the performer was liable.

CARILLONEUR, (*F.*) a performer on the *carillons*.

CARTA, (abbreviated *car.* or *cart*,) used by the Italians for page or folio.

CAREZZANDO, (*I.*) in a caressing or coaxing style.

CARICATO, (*I.*) in a caricatured or exaggerated manner.

CARILLONS, (*F.*) chimes, consisting of bells diatonically tuned, on which airs are played by clock-work.

CARITA, CON CARITA, (*I.*) with tenderness.

CAROL, the name applied to the old ballads sung at Christmas by itinerant minstrels.

CARRATTERE, (*I.*) character; as, *con molto carrattere*, with much character.

CARACTERES DE MUSIQUE, a French term applied to musical signs collectively.

CAROLA, (*I.*) synonymous with *ballata*; a simple song sung to a dance.

CASSA, chest or box.

—— **GRANDE**, (*I.*) the great drum in military music.

CASTAGNETS, or **CASTANETS**, hollow shells used to accompany dance tunes in Spain and other southern countries.

CASTANETAS, }
CASTANUELAS, } (*S.*) the castagnets or castanets.

CASTORION, a melody performed by the Greeks just previous to an attack.

CASTRATO, an artificially formed soprano or treble singer.

CATACOUSTICS, that part of acoustics which considers the property of sounds and echoes.

CATTIVO, bad, unfit; as, *cattivo tempo* is a certain part or time of the measure, whereon it is not proper to perform certain things; as, to end a cadence, place a long syllable, &c.

CATCH, a humorous composition for three or four voices, so contrived that the singers catch up each other's sentences.

CATENA DI TRILLI, (*I.*) a chain or succession of shakes.

CAUDA. See *Coda* and *Virgula.*

CAVALQUET, or LE MARCHE, a trumpet signal for the march of cavalry.

CAVATA, a small song, sometimes preceded by a recitative.

CAVATINA, (*I.*) an air of one movement or part only, occasionally preceded by a recitative.

C BARRÉ, (*F.*) the character ₵ indicating *alla breve* time.

C DUR, (*G.*) the key of C major.

CEBELL, the name of an old air written in common time.

CELERE, (*I.*) quick, rapid.

CELERITA, *con,* (*I.*) with celerity, quick.

CELESTE, (*F.*) indicates the employment of the pedal, in some piano-fortes, which acts on the celestina, or soft stop.

CEMBALO, (*I.*) the harpsichord.

CENTONE, a sort of medley on a large scale, being several tunes connected by appropriate passages.

CEPHALICAS, the name of one of the musical characters of notation used in the middle ages.

CERVALET, a short wind instrument.

CES, (*G.*) C flat.

CHACONNE, (*F.*) an air constructed on a ground bass; a Spanish dance.

CHALUMEAU, (*F.*) an ancient rustic flute. When this word occurs in music written for the clarinet, it signifies that the passage to which it refers must be played an octave lower.

CHANGEABLE, said of those chants which may be performed either in the major or minor key of the tonic in which they are written.

CHANGING NOTES, passing notes on the accented parts of a bar.

CHANSON, (*F.*) a song.

CHANSONNETTE, (*F.*) a short or little song.

CHANSONS DE GESTE, (*F.*) historical romances, sung by minstrels of the 13th century.

CHANT, a simple melody, generally harmonized in four parts, to which the daily psalms are sung in cathedrals, &c. See *Single Chant* and *Double Chant.*

CHANT, (*F.*) a song or melody, the vocal part.

CHANT GREGORIEN, (*F.*) the Gregorian Chant.

CHANT SUR LE LIVRE, (*F.*) a barbarous kind of counterpoint on the plain chant, performed by several voices, each singing extempore.

CHANTANT, (*F.*) in a singing manner.

CHANTERELLE, (*F.*) the first string of the violin or guitar.

CHANTEUR, (*F.*) a male vocalist.

CHANTEUSE, (*F.*) a female vocalist.

CHANT EN ISON, psalmody of only two notes.

CHANTRE, (*F.*) the leader of a choir.

CHANTERRES, Provencial singers of songs and ballads.

CHANTRY PRIESTS, certain stipendiary priests, whose particular office it was to sing mass in the *chantries.*

CHANTRIES, institutions in the Romish church, endowed for the purpose of singing masses for the founders.

CHAMADE, a beat of the drum, or sound of trumpet, to indicate to an enemy a willingness to capitulate, make a truce, or the like.

CHASSE, (*F.*) in the hunting style.

CHE, (*I.*) than; as, *poco più che andante,* a little slower than *andante.*

CHELYS, (*Gk.*) a stringed instrument of the lute species.

CHEVALET, (*F.*) the bridge of any instrument of the violin species.

CHEVILLE, (*F.*) the peg of a violin, tenor, violoncello, &c.

CHERUBICAL HYMN, a hymn of great note in the early Christian church.

CHEST OF VIOLS, an old expression applied to a set of viols, consisting of six, the particular use of which was to play fantasias in six parts.

CHIAREZZA, *con,* (*I.*) with clearness and neatness.

CHIARO, (*I.*) clear, as regards sound or tone.

CHIAROSCURO, (*I.*) light and shade, in modifications of *forte* and *piano.*

CHIAVE, (*I.*) a clef or key.

CHIROGYMNASTE, a square board on which are placed various mechanical contrivances for exercising the fingers of the pianist.

CHIESA, (*I.*) church; as, *musica di chiesa,* music for the church.

CHIFFRES, (*F.*) figures, in speaking of thorough-bass.

CHIROPLAST, an instrument for the guidance of the hands and fingers of young practitioners on the piano-forte.

CHIUDENDO, (*I.*) concluding; as, *chiudendo col motivo*, concluding with the subject.

CHITARRA, (*I.*) a guitar.

CHIMES, a kind of periodical music on bells, produced at equal intervals by means of an apparatus added to a clock, or by a regular performer.

CHO, Scotch name for a double trumpet having great power of tone.

CHŒUR, (*F.*) the choir, or chorus.

CHOIR, that portion of a chapel or cathedral set apart for the singers in divine worship; as also the singers themselves, taken collectively.

CHOIR ORGAN, the smaller or softer toned organ, used to accompany the principal singers in solos, duets, &c.

CHOR, (*G.*) choir, chorus; as, *arie und chor*, air and chorus.

CHORAL, belonging to the choir; full, or for many voices.

CHORAL, (*G.*) a psalm tune.

CHORALMASSIG, (*G.*) in the style of a psalm tune.

CHORD, a combination of several sounds forming harmony.

CHORDOMETER, an instrument by which to ascertain the strength of strings.

CHORIAMBUS, a musical foot, accented thus: — ⌣ ⌣ —.

CHORISTER, the leader of a choir.

CHORUS, a band or company of singers.

CHORSÄNGER, (*G.*) a chorus singer.

CHORIST, a member of a choir.

CHORION, a Greek composition, consisting of a hymn sung in honor of Cybele, the mother of the heathen gods.

CHORO-FAVORITO, (*I.*) a chorus in which the best voices and instruments are employed.

——— RECITANTE, same as *Choro-Favorito.*

CHROMA, a term signifying a graceful style of singing.

CHROMATIC, proceeding by semitones, or formed by means of semitones.

CHROMATIQUE, (*F.*) chromatic, proceeding by semitones.

CHURCH MODES, the ancient modes called by the following names: Dorian, Phrygian, Lydian, Mixolydian, Æolian, Ionian or Iastian.

CIACONNE, (*I.*) a *chaconne*, a Spanish dance.

CIMBALLES, (*F. Pl.*) cymbals, a military instrument.

CINQUE, a composition intended for five voices.

CIS, (*G.*) C sharp; as,

—— **DUR**, C sharp major.

—— **MOLL**, C sharp minor.

CISCIS, (*G.*) C double sharp.

CITHARA, an ancient instrument of the harp kind.

———— **HISPANICA**, Spanish guitar.

CITHARISTIC, music intended for the harp or guitar.

CITTAM, old English name of the guitar.

CITOLE, an instrument of the dulcimer species, and probably synonymous with it.

CITTERN, an old instrument resembling the lute.

CIVETTERIA, (*I.*) coquettishly.

CLARIBELLA, the name of an organ stop tuned in unison with the diapasons.

CLARICHORD, } **CLAVICHORD**, } a small keyed instrument of the spinet kind.

CLARINET, a wind instrument blown with a reed.

CLARINETTO, (*I.*) the clarinet.

CLARINETTISTA, } **CLARINETTISTE**, } (*I.*) a performer on the clarinet.

CLARINO, (*I.*) the Italian name for trumpet.

————, (*I.*) } **CLARION**, (*F.*) } an octave trumpet, an organ stop so called.

CLANGOR, a loud, shrill sound, peculiar to the trumpet.

———— **TUBARUM**, an old Roman trumpet.

CLAPPER, a piece of metal suspended in a bell, which, striking the lower end of the barrel, produces the sound.

CLAUSULA AFFINALIS, (*L.*) a cadence in a key related to the predominant one of the piece.

———— **DISSECTA**, (*L.*) half cadence.

———— **PEREGRINA**, (*L.*) a cadence in a key the fundamental tone of which is not in the scale of the principal key.

———— **PRIMARIA**, (*L.*) the cadence in the principal key.

———— **SECUNDARIA**, (*L.*) the cadence in the fifth.

———— **MEDIANS**, the cadence in a minor key when in the key of a third.

CLAVIER, (*F., G.*) the key-board of a piano or organ.

CLAVECIN, (*F.*) a harpsichord.

CLAVICEMBALO, (*I.*) **CLAVICEMBALUM**, (*L.*) the harpsichord.

CLAVES SIGNATÆ, a term applied to a key which was marked, and thus became the fundamental note of the scale.

CLAVIS, (*L.*) a key.

CLAVIOTHERIUM, an ancient, oblong, keyed instrument.

CLEFS, characters serving to determine the names and acuteness or gravity of every note in the stave to which they are prefixed.

CLEF DE FA, (*F.*) the F, or bass clef, marked thus, 

——— **SOL**, (*F.*) the G, or treble clef, 

—— **D'UT**, (*F.*) the C clef, 

CLINIS, name given by the Greek musicians of the middle ages to one of their notes.

CLOCHETTE, (*F.*) a little bell.

CLORONE, a species of clarinet which is a fifth lower than the C clarinet.

CLOSE PLAIN SHAKE, that of a semitone, rapid, though with less energy than the open shake.

——— **TURNED SHAKE**, that which ends with a turn.

C MOLL, (*G.*) C minor.

CODA, (*I.*) a few bars added at the close of a composition, beyond its natural termination.

CODETTA, (*I.*) a short passage serving to connect one period or movement with another.

COI, (*Pl.*) **COL**, **COLL'**, **COLLA**, **COLLO**, (*I.*) with the.

COI VIOLINI, (*I.*) with the violins.

COL ARCO, a mark in a piece to indicate the use of the bow.

—— **BASSO**, (*I.*) with the bass.

—— **LEGNO DELL' ARCO**, (*I.*) with the bow-stick.

—— **CANTO**, **COLLA VOCE**, (*I.*) with the melody or voice. These expressions imply that the accompanist must follow the singer in regard to time.

COLLA PARTE, (*I.*) implies that the accompanist must follow the principal part in regard to time.

COLL' ARCO, (*I.*) with the bow.

COLOFONIA, (*I.*) }
COLOPHON, (*F.*) } resin.

COLLA PUNTA DELL ARCO, employ the point of the bow.

COLORATURA, every variety of musical ornament.

COME, (*I.*) as.

——— **PRIMA,** (*I.*) as before.

——— **SOPRA,** (*I.*) as above or before.

——— **STA,** (*I.*) as it stands.

COMES, (*L.*) the answer of a fugue.

COMMA, (*I.*) a small interval, treated of in the doctrine of musical ratios.

COMMENÇANT, (*F.*) a beginner in music, &c.

COMMODO, *con,* }
COMMODAMENTE, } (*I.*) quietly, with composure.

COMMON CHORD, a chord consisting of a bass note together with its third and fifth, to which the octave is often added.

———— **TIMES,** those which have an even number of parts in a bar.

COMPASS, the range of notes comprehended by any voice or instrument.

COMPIACEVOLE, (*I.*) pleasing, attractive.

COMPIACEVOLMENTE, in a pleasant and agreeable style.

COMPIETA, a psalm or hymn used in the Romish church service.

COMPLIN, (*L.*) evening service during Lent, in the Catholic church.

COMPOSITEUR, (*F.*) }
COMPOSITORE, (*I.*) } a composer.

COMPOSITION. Any musical production is so called. The art of inventing music.

COMPONERE, (*I.*) to compose.

COMPOSURA, (*L.*) a composition.

COMPOSIZIONE, (*I.*) a musical composition.

COMPOSIZIONE DI TAVOLINO, (*I.*) table music; as, glees, catches, &c.

COMPOSTO, (*I.*) composed.

COMPOUND INTERVALS, such as exceed the extent of an octave.

———— TIMES, those measures which contain two or three principal accents; as, $\frac{6}{8}$, $\frac{12}{8}$, $\frac{9}{8}$, &c.

———— COMMON TIME, a time containing six quarter or six eighth notes in a measure.

———— TRIPLE TIME, a time with nine quarter or eighth notes in a measure.

COMPONISTA, a composer of music.

COMPUTATRICES, (*L.*) name given to those women whom the ancients hired to sing and weep over the dead at funerals.

COMPLEMENT, that quantity which is wanting to any interval to fill up the octave.

CON, (*I.*) with.

—— AFFETTO, (*I.*) in an affecting manner.

—— AFFLIZIONE, } (*I.*) with affliction and distress.
—— AMAREZZA, }

—— ANIMA, (*I.*) with animation and feeling.

—— AUDACE, (*I.*) with boldness.

—— BRIO, (*I.*) with brilliancy and spirit.

—— CELERITA, (*I.*) with quickness.

—— COMMODO, (*I.*) in a convenient degree of movement.

—— DILIGENZA, (*I.*) diligently, in a studied manner.

—— DELICATEZZA, (*I.*) with peculiar sweetness.

—— DOLCE MANIERA, (*I.*) in a simple, delicate manner.

—— DISCREZIONE, (*I.*) with discretion.

—— DISPERAZIONE, (*I.*) with despair.

—— DOLCEZZA, (*I.*) with sweetness.

—— DOLORE, } (*I.*) mournfully, with grief and pathos.
—— DUOLO, }

—— ELEGANZA, (*I.*) with elegance.

—— ENERGIA, (*I.*) with energy.

—— ENTUSIASMO, (*I.*) with enthusiasm.

—— ESPRESSIONE, (*I.*) with expression.

—— FACILITA, (*I.*) with facility.

—— FORZA, (*I.*) with force, vehemently.

—— FUOCO, (*I.*) with fire and animation.

—— FURIA, (*I.*) furiously, with vehemence.

—— FLESSIBILITA, (*I.*) flexible, unconstrained.

CON GENTILEZZA, (*I.*) with grace and elegance.
—— GIUSTEZZA, (*I.*) with precision.
———————— DELL' INTONAZIONE, (*I.*) with appropriate intonation.
—— GRAVITA, (*I.*) with gravity.
—— GRAZIA, (*I.*) with grace and elegance.
—— GUSTO, GUSTOSO, (*I.*) tastefully.
—— IMPETO, (*I.*) with force.
————— DOLOROSO, (*I.*) with pathetic force and energy.
—— INDIFFERENSA, in an easy, indifferent manner.
—— INNOCENZA, (*I.*) in an artless and innocent style.
—— JUSTO, (*I.*) with exact precision.
—— LEGGIEREZZA, (*I.*) with lightness and delicacy.
—— LENTEZZA, (*I.*) with slowness.
—— MISTERO, (*I.*) with an air of mystery.
—— MODERAZIONE, (*I.*) with a moderate degree of quickness.
—— MOLTO PASSIONE, (*I.*) in a highly feeling and affecting style.
————— SENTIMENTO, (*I.*) with much feeling or sentiment.
—— MORBIDEZZA, (*I.*) with excess of delicacy.
—— MOTO, (*I.*) with somewhat of an agitated expression.
—— NEGLIGENZA, (*I.*) negligently, without restraint.
—— OSSERVANZA, (*I.*) with scrupulous exactness in regard to time.
—— PIACEVOLEZZA, (*I.*) in a pleasing and graceful style.
—— PRECIPITAZIONE, (*I.*) in a hurried manner.
—— PRECISIONE, (*I.*) with distinctness and precision.
—— PRESTEZZA, (*I.*) with rapidity.
—— RABBIA, (*I.*) with rage, furiously.
—— RAPIDITA, (*I.*) with rapidity.
—— RISOLUZIONE, (*I.*) with boldness and resolution.
—— SDEGNO, (*I.*) in a fiery and indignant style.
—— SEMPLICITA, (*I.*) with simplicity.
—— SENSIBILITA, (*I.*) with sensibility and feeling.
—— SENTIMENTO, (*I.*) with feeling and sentiment.
—— STRUMENTI, (*I.*) a performance with voices and instruments united.
—— SONORITA, (*I.*) with a full, vibrating kind of tone.

CON SORDINI, (*I.*) with mutes.
—— SPIRITO, (*I.*) with quickness and spirit.
—— SOLENNITA, (*I.*) with solemnity.
—— SUAVITA, (*I.*) with sweetness and delicacy.
—— TENEREZZA, (*I.*) with tenderness.
—— TEPIDITA, (*I.*) with coldness and indifference.
—— TIMIDEZZA, (*I.*) with timidity.
—— VARIAZIONE, (*I.*) with variations.
—— VEEMENZA, (*I.*) forcibly, vehemently.
—— VIOLENZA, (*I.*) with violence.
—— VIVEZZA, (*I.*) with animation, vivaciously.
—— ZELO, (*I.*) with zeal.

CONCENTO, (*I.*) concord, the consonance of voices and instruments.

CONCENTRARE, (*I.*) to concentrate the sounds.

CONCERT, a musical performance, in which several persons are engaged.

CONCERTANTE, (*I.*) a piece of music for an orchestra, in which several of the instruments have occasional solos. It is also used adjectively; as, *duo concertante*, a duet in which each part is alternately principal and subordinate.

CONCERTINA, (*I.*) a small sexangular musical instrument held in the hands. The sounds are produced from metal tongues by pressing the fingers upon the keys, which are situated on both sides of the instrument, and at the same time moving the bellows, to obtain the necessary supply of wind.

CONCERTINO, (*I.*) This term always denotes a principal part in a concerto, or other full piece; as, *violino primo concertino*, first principal violin; *violino secondo concertino*, second principal violin.

CONCERTO, (*I.*) a composition intended to display the powers of some particular instrument, with orchestral accompaniments.

CONCERTO GROSSO, (*I.*) a composition for many instruments, some principal, some auxiliary.

———— SPIRITUALE, (*I.*) a miscellaneous concert, chiefly of sacred music.

CONCERT-SPIELER, (*G.*) a solo-player.

————STÜCK, (*G.*) a concerted piece, a concerto.

CONCINNOUS, harmonizing, coinciding in effect.

4

CONCITATO, (*I.*) perturbed, agitated.

CONCORD, an agreeable combination of sounds.

CONNOISSEUR, (*F.*) a skilful judge and lover of music.

CONSECUTIVE, a term applied to a series of similar intervals or chords.

CONSEQUENT, the answer of a fugue, or of a point of imitation.

CONSERVATOIRE, (*F.*)
CONSERVATORIO, (*I.*) } a public school of music.

CONSOLANTE, (*I.*) in a cheering and encouraging manner.

CONSONANT, those parts which harmonize well with each other.

CONSONANCE, an interval agreeable to the ear.

CONTINUATO, (*I.*) continued or held down or on, speaking of notes.

CONTRA-BASSO, (*I.*) the double bass.

———FAGOTTO, (*I.*) double bassoon.

CONTRALTO, (*I.*) a counter-tenor voice. The highest species of male voice, and the lowest of female voices.

CONTRAPUNCKT, (*G.*) counterpoint.

CONTRAPUNTISTA, (*I.*) one who understands counterpoint.

CONTRAPUNTO, (*I.*) counterpoint, the first and most necessary step towards a knowledge of musical composition.

——— SOPRA IL SOGETTO, (*I.*) counterpoint above the subject.

——— SOTTO IL SOGETTO, (*I.*) counterpoint below the subject.

——— ALLA MENTE, (*I.*) See *Chant sur le Livre.*

——— DOPPIO, (*I.*) double counterpoint.

CONTRASSOGGETTO, (*I.*) the counter-subject of a fugue.

CONTRASPORTO, (*I.*) in an angry and passionate manner.

CONTREPOINT, (*F.*) counterpoint.

CONTREPOINTISTE, (*F.*) a contrapuntist.

CONTRESUJET, (*F.*) the counter-subject of a fugue.

CONTRETEMPS, (*F.*) syncopation — driving notes, or unaccented and accented notes tied together, contrary to the natural rhythmic flow of the measure.

CONTRARY MOTION, motion in an opposite direction to some other part.

CONTRA VIOLONE, (*I.*) the double bass.

CONTRE-BASSE, (*F.*) a double bass.

——DANSE, (*F.*) a quadrille or country-dance.

——TEMS, (*F.*) a change from the time.

CONTINUED HARMONY, a harmony which does not change, though the bass varies.

CONTINUO, (*I.*) without cessation.

CONTRA, (*I.*) low, under, counter.

CONTRO, (*I.*) counter, low or lower.

CONTRADDANZA, counter-dance.

CONTRARCO, a reversed movement of the bow.

CONJUNCT, (*Gk.*) employed by the ancients to denote those two tetrachords which formed the modern scale.

CONDUCTOR, a person who arranges, orders, and directs the necessary preparations for a concert, and also superintends and conducts the performance.

CONDUCTUS, (*L.*) a species of air much used in the time of Franco.

COPULA, (*L.*) that movement in an organ by which two rows of keys can be connected together, or the pedals with the keys.

COPERTO, to deaden the sound either by covering or otherwise.

CORNMUSE, a Cornish pipe, similar to a bagpipe.

CORANTO, (*I.*) a certain air comprising three crotchets in a bar.

COROMEION, (*Gk.*) a brazen bell much used by the ancients.

CORDATURA, the system by which stringed instruments are tuned.

CORODICA, a vocal performance by more than one voice.

CORONET, a hold.

COR, (*F.*) a horn.

CORALE, (*I.*) the plain chant.

CORANTE, (*I.*) a slow dance in $\frac{3}{2}$ or $\frac{3}{4}$ time.

CORDA, (*I.*) } a string; as, *sopra una corda*, or *sur une corde*, on
CORDE, (*F.*) } one string.

COR DE CHASSE, (*F.*) a French horn.

—— SIGNAL, (*F.*) a bugle.

CORDIERA, (*I.*) the tail-piece of a violin, tenor, &c.

CORIPHŒUS, (*L.*) the leader of the dances.

CORNAMUSA, (*I.*) the bagpipe.

CORNET, the name of an organ stop consisting of several ranks of pipes.

CORNET,
CORNETTO, } (*I.*) a pipe or English flute.
CORNET A PISTONS, (*F.*) a species of trumpet with valves.
CORNETTINO, (*I.*) a small cornet.
CORNIST, a performer on the horn.
CORNI, (*I.*) the horns.
CORNO, (*I.*) a horn.
——— DI BASSETTO, (*I.*) a basset horn.
——— DI CACCIA, (*I.*) a French horn.
——— INGLESE, (*I.*) an English horn.
CORO, (*I.*) a chorus, or piece for many voices.
CORONA, (*I.*) a pause, marked 𝄐.
CORRENTE, (*I.*) an old dance tune in triple time.
CORYPHÉE, (*F.*) the leader of the groups of dancers.
COTILLON, (*F.*) a lively and animated dance in $\frac{6}{8}$ time.
COUNTER-FUGUE, a fugue in which the subjects move in contrary directions.
————TENOR, the highest adult male voice, and the lowest female voice.
———————— CLEF, the clef placed on the third line in order to accommodate the counter-tenor voice.
———————— VOICE, that male voice which ranks in height next above the tenor voice; also the lowest female voice.
COUNTERPOINT, the art of composition.
COUNTRY-DANCE, a lively, pointed air, calculated for dancing. It is not confined to any particular measure, so that any common song or tune, if cheerful, may become a country-dance.
COUPS D'ARCHET, (*F.*) strokes of the bow, ways of bowing.
COULÉ, (*F.*) a group of two notes connected by a slur.
COUCHED HARP, the spinet.
COURANTE, (*F.*) an antiquated dance tune in triple time, examples of which are to be found in Corelli, Handel, Seb. Bach, &c.
COVERED CONSECUTIVES. See *Hidden Consecutives.*
CREDO, (*L.*) one of the movements of the Catholic service, commencing with that word; the Belief.
CREMONA, (*I.*) a small town in Italy, remarkable as having been the dwelling-place of several of the greatest violin-makers, as Amati, Straduarius, Guarnarius, &c. Also, an organ stop.

CRESCENDO, (*I.*) a word intimating a gradual increase of loudness; sometimes expressed thus <.

——— **E INCALCANDO POCO-A-POCO,** (*I.*) increasing and hastening by degrees.

——— **POCO-A-POCO,** (*I.*) to increase the sound little by little.

——— **POI DIMINUENDO,** (*I.*) increasing and then diminishing the sound.

CREMORN, or **CREMORNE,** an organ stop of eight feet, of the reed kind, sometimes called *cremona.*

CROCHE, (*F.*) }
CROMA, (*I.*) } a quaver.

CROOKS, small tubes applied to trumpets, horns, &c., to change their pitch and adapt them to the key of the piece in which they are to be used.

CROTCHET, a note of which the length is one half that of the minim in the same piece.

CROMATICA, (*I.*) chromatic.

CROWLE, an English wind instrument of former times, a kind of base flute or bassoon.

CROTALUM, (*Gk.*) an ancient instrument.

CRUCIFIXUS EST, (*L.*) part of the Credo in the Catholic service.

CRWTH, a singular Welsh instrument with six strings, and played upon with a bow.

C SCHLÜSSEL, (*G.*) the C clef.

CUM SANCTO SPIRITU, (*L.*) part of the Gloria.

——— **CANTU,** or **CUM DIOCANTU,** with vocal melody.

CUSTOS, (*L.*) a direct.

CYMBALS, those metal plates used in military bands, and which on being struck together produce a clashing sound.

CYMBALUM, an instrument of antiquity, similar to the tympanum or drum.

D.

DA, (*I.*) by, for, from, &c.

DA CAMERA, (*I.*) in the style of chamber music.

DA CAPELLA, (*I.*) in the church style.

DA CAPO, or **D. C.,** (*I.*) from the beginning. An expression which is often written at the end of a movement, to indicate that the performer must return to and finish with the first strain.

DA CAPO AL FINE, (*I.*) an expression placed at the end of a movement, signifying that the performer must return to the first part, and conclude where the word *fine* is placed.

DACTYL, a musical foot composed of one long and two short notes.

DACTYLION, a machine invented by H. Herz, for strengthening the fingers, and rendering them independent in piano-forte playing.

DAL, (*I.*), by; as, *dal segno*, from the sign; a mark of repetition.

—— TEATRO, (*I.*) in the style of theatrical music.

DAMPERS, certain movable parts in the internal frame of a piano-forte, which are covered with cloth, and by means of a pedal are brought into contact with the wires, in order to deaden the vibration.

DAMPER PEDAL, that pedal of a piano-forte which raises the dampers from the strings, and thus allows them their full continuous vibration. In piano-forte music, the word *ped.*, or the character ⊕, is used to indicate when the damper pedal is to be used.

DANCERIE, a collection of dance tunes.

DANCES, certain tunes composed for, or used in dancing; as, the waltz, minuet, cotillon, reel, hornpipe, &c.

DANSE, (*F.*) a dance.

DA TEATRO, (*I.*) for the theatre.

DAUER, (*G.*) the duration or length of notes.

D DUR, (*G.*) D major.

DEBILE, (*I.*) weakly, faintly.

DEBOLE, (*I.*) feebly.

DECANI, (*L. Pl.*) priests. In cathedral music, this term is used to indicate those passages that are to be sung by those singers only who are in holy orders.

DECISO, (*I.*) in a bold, decided manner.

DECISSIMO, (*I.*) with greatest decision and firmness of touch.

DECKE, (*G.*) the bell of a violin, violoncello, &c.

DECORATION, (*F.*) a term used by some French theorists in the sense of *signature*.

DECRESCENDO, (*I.*) diminishing the intensity or force of the sound.

DECEPTIVE MODULATION, that which leads to an unexpected melody.

DECLAMANDO, in the recitative style.

DEGREE, (ACADEMIC,) an honor conferred by a university.

DEGREE, (THEORETICAL,) the difference of position or elevation between two notes.

DEGRE, (*F.*) a step or degree of the stave.

DELIBERATAMENTE, } deliberately.
DELIBERATO, }

DELL', DELLA, DELLO, (*I.*) of the.

DELICATO, DELICATEMENTE, } (*I.*) delicately.
DELICATEZZA, *con*, }

DELICATISSIMO, (*I.*) with extreme delicacy.

DELYN, the name given by the Welsh to their harp.

DELASSEMENT, a musical exercise, pleasing and attractive.

DEMANCHER, (*F.*) to change the position of the hand on the guitar, violin, &c.

DEMI, (*F.*) a half.

DEMI-CADENCE, (*I.*) a half-cadence in harmony.

———DITONE, (*F.*) a minor third.

———PAUSE, (*F.*) a minim rest.

DEMIQUART DE SOUPIR, (*F.*) a demisemiquaver rest.

DEMISEMIQUAVER, a short note, equal in duration to one half the semiquaver.

DEMI-SOUPIR, (*F.*) a quaver rest.

——— TON, (*F.*) a semitone.

DE PROFUNDIS, (*L.*) one of the seven penitential psalms.

DEPLORATION, a dirge, or any mournful strain.

DERIVATIVES, chords derived from others by inversion.

DES, (*G.*) D flat.

DESCANT, an extemporaneous or other counterpoint on a given subject.

DESCENDANT, (*F.*) in descending.

DES DUR, (*G.*) D flat major.

DES MOLL, D flat minor.

DESSUS, (*F.*) the treble or upper vocal part.

DESTRA, (*I.*) } the right hand.
DEXTRA, (*L.*) }

DESCENDING, passing from any note to one less acute.

DESCENT, the lowering of the tone of a voice or instrument.

DÉTACHÉ, (*F.*) staccato.

DETERMINATO, a delivery in exact time, and given firm and decided.

DEUTSCHE FLOTE, (*G.*) a German flute.

DEUTEROS, (*Gk.*) second; the numerical term by which the ancients marked the Æolian mode.

DEXTRÆ, (*L.*) Romans who played on two flutes at the same time.

DI, (*I.*) of.

DIA, (*Gk.*) through.

DIALOGO, (*I.*) a dialogue. A piece or passage in which two or more parts are so constructed as to respond to one another.

DIAPASON, an octave; a term applied to certain essential stops in an organ, which extend throughout the whole scale of the instrument. Of these there are several sorts; as, open diapason, stopped diapason, double diapason, &c.

DIAPENTE, (*Gk.*) a perfect fifth.

DIATESSERON, (*Gk.*) a perfect fourth.

DIATONIC, (*Gk.*) naturally; that is, according to the degrees of the major or minor scale, or by tones and semitones only.

DIACONICON, the book of service used by the Greek church.

DIAGRAMMA, (*Gk.*) diagram, the score.

DIAPHONIA, rules for the use of the organ in connection with vocal music.

DIAPHONA, a composition for two voices.

DIAPHONICA, (*Gk.*) a dissonant interval.

DIASTEMA, (*Gk.*) interval.

DIATONIC SCALE, the seven gradations of tone, arranged in conformity with some particular key.

DIAZEUXIS, (*Gk.*) division; name given by the ancients to the tone which separates two disjunct tetrachords.

DIAPENTISSARE, a method of descant by fifths.

DIACHISMA, (*Gk.*) an interval in ancient music, forming the half of a minor semitone.

DIASTALTIC, (*Gk.*) dilating.

DIASTEM, an interval or space.

DIATESSARONARE, (*Gk.*) an expression implying singing in fourths.

DIATONUM INTENSUM, the name given by musical theorists to those famous proportions of the intervals proposed by Ptolemy in his system of that name.

DICHORD, (*Gk.*) a two-stringed lyre.

DIESARE, (*I.*) } to raise the pitch of a note by means of a
DIÉSER, (*F.*) } sharp.

DIES IRÆ, (*L.*) a principal movement in a requiem.

DIESIS, (*Gk.*) a small interval used in the mathematical computations of intervals.

DIEZE, (*F.*) a sharp.

DIEZEUGMENON, (*Gk.*) the third tetrachord disjoined from the second.

DI GRADO, (*I.*) by degrees, in opposition to moving by skips.

———— **ASCENDENTE**, a series of notes of regular ascent.

———— **DESCENDENTE**, a series of notes of regular descent.

DI GRADE, a regular succession of notes according to the scale.

— **MOLTO**, (*I.*) an expression which serves to augment the signification of the word to which it is added; as, *allegro di molto*, very quick.

— **SALTO**, (*I.*) a term applied to melody. See *Salto*.

DIGRESSIONE, a deviation from the regular course of the piece.

DILETTANTE, (*F.*) a lover of music.

DILUENDO, (*I.*) a gradual dying away of the tone till it arrives at extinction.

DIMINISHED, somewhat less than perfect, as applied to intervals, chords, &c.

———— **INTERVALS**, such intervals as are a chromatic semitone less than the corresponding perfect or minor intervals.

DIMINUÉ, (*F.*) } diminished, in regard to intervals and chords.
DIMINUITO, (*I.*) }

DIMINUTION, imitation of a given subject by means of notes of shorter duration.

DIMINUENDO or **DIM.**, (*I.*) This term implies that the quantity or intensity of tone must be gradually diminished.

D' INGANNO, an unexpected ending.

DIRECT, a character placed at the end of a stave, to apprise the performer of the first note in the succeeding stave.

——— **MOTION**, synonymous with parallel or similar motion.

DIRECTEUR, (*F.*) the director or conductor of a musical performance.

DIRGE, a funeral song.

DIRETTORE DELLA MUSICA, a director of a musical performance.

DIRITTA, the gradual rise or fall of the voice.

DISEURS, (*F.*) those who in a kind of chant recited their metrical histories.

DISCRETO, with discretion.

DISTENDENTE, changes in the course of a piece.

DISCANT. See *Descant*. It also implies the upper part.

——— CLEF, treble or soprano clef.

DISCORD, a dissonant combination of sounds.

DIS-DIAPASON, a double octave.

——-MOLL, (*G.*) D sharp minor.

D MOLL, (*G.*) D minor.

DISPERATO, } (*I.*) despairingly, with extreme emotion.
DISPERAZIONE, *con*, }

DISPERSED HARMONY, harmony in which the notes forming the different chords are separated from each other by wide intervals.

DISSONANCE, an interval or chord displeasing to the ear.

DISSONANT, an inharmonious combination of sounds.

DITO, (*I.*) the finger.

DITONE, (*I.*) } the major third or interval of two whole tones.
DITONUS, (*L.*) }

DITHYRAMBICS, (*Gk.*) songs in honor of Bacchus.

DIVERBIA, the dramatic dialogues of the ancients.

DIVERTIMENTO, (*I.*) a short, light composition, written in a familiar and pleasing style.

DIVERTISSEMENT, (*F.*) certain airs and dances resembling a short ballet, introduced between the acts of the French or Italian opera. Also, a composition in a light and pleasing style.

DIVISI, (*I. Pl.*) This word is occasionally met with in orchestral parts, when a passage is written in octaves or other intervals. It implies that one half of the performers must play the upper notes, and the others the lower ones.

DIVISION, a series of notes sung to one syllable. Formerly, this term implied a kind of variation upon a given subject.

DIVOTO, (*I.*) devoutly, in a solemn style.

DIVOZIONE, *con*, (*I.*) with religious feeling.

DO, (*I.*) a syllable applied in solfaing to the note C.

DOCTOR OF MUSIC, a degree conferred by one of the universities.

DODECACHORDON, (*Gk.*) the twelve modes of Aristoxenus.

DOIGTE, (*F.*) fingered.

DOIGTER, (*F.*) the fingering.

DOLCE, or DOL., (*I.*) implies a soft and sweet style of performance.

——— CON GUSTO, in a soft, sweet style.

——— E LUSINGANDO, with a peculiar soft and attractive expression.

——— MA MARCATO, delicate and gentle, yet decided.

——— MANIERA, (*I.*) a sweet, delicate, and finished style of performance.

DOLCIANO, DOLCINO, DULCIAN, DULCINO, (*I.*) a small bassoon, formerly much in use.

DOLENTE, (*I.*) grieving, mournful.

DOLENTEMENTE, (*I.*) plaintively, mournfully.

DOLENTISSIMO, (*I.*) the superlative of *dolente.*

DOLORE, CON DOLORE, (*I.*) with grief.

DOLOROSO, DOLOROSAMENTE, (*I.*) dolorously.

DOLCEMENTE, (*I.*) in a sweet and graceful style.

DOLCEZZA, or CON DOLCEZZA, (*I.*) with sweetness and softness.

DOLCISSIMO, (*I.*) with extreme sweetness.

DOMINANT, a name given by theorists to the fifth note of the scale.

DOMINANTE, (*F.*) the dominant or fifth note of the scale, so called from its governing the key-note in harmony.

DOMINE SALVUM FAC, (*L.*) a prayer for the king, sung after the mass.

DOMESTICI, (*L.*) an assistant in the patriarchal church of Constantinople.

DOPPO, (*I.*) after.

DOPPEL, (*G.*) double; as,

DOPPELGRIFFE, (*G.*) double stop on the violin, &c.

DOPPELSCHLAG, (*G.*) a turn.

DOPPIO, (*I.*) double.

DOPPIO MOVIMENTO, (*I.*) double time; that is, as fast again.
——— TEMPO, (*I.*) double time.

DORIAN, the name of one of the ancient modes.

DOT, a character which, when placed after a note or rest, increases its duration by the half of its original value.

DOUBLE, an old term for a variation used by Scarlatti and others.
——— A. Any capital letter doubled indicates that the tone is an octave lower than when single.
——— BEMOL, (*F.*) double flat.
——— BAR, two thick strokes drawn through the staff.
——— CHANT, a simple harmonized melody extending to two verses of a psalm as sung in cathedrals, &c.
——— COUNTERPOINT, a counterpoint which admits of the parts being inverted.
——— CROCHE, (*F.*) a semiquaver.
——— BASS, a large, deep-toned bass instrument.
——— DIEZE, (*F.*) double sharp.
——— DOT. Two dots placed after a note increase its duration three fourths of its original length.
——— DRUM, a large drum used in military bands, and beaten at both ends.
——— FUGUE, a fugue on two subjects.
——— TONGUEING, a mode of articulating quick notes, used by flutists.

DOUBLETTE, (*F.*) an organ stop, called by us the fifteenth.

DOUX, (*F.*) softly, sweetly.

DRAGG, or STRASCINO, a grace, consisting of descending notes.

DRAMA, DRAME, (*F.*) DRAMMA, (*I.*) } a poem accommodated to action; a play, a comedy, a tragedy.

DRAMATIQUE, (*F.*) DRAMMATICO, (*I.*) } dramatic.

DRAMMA BURLESCA, (*I.*) a comic or humorous drama.

DREYKLANG, (*G.*) a chord of three sounds, a triad.

DREYSTIMMIG, (*G.*) in three parts.

DRITTA, (*I.*) right; as, *mano dritta*, the right hand.

DRIVING NOTES. This term is sometimes applied to long notes when placed between shorter notes, and accented contrary to the natural rhythmic flow of melody.

DROITE, (*F.*) right; as, *maine droite*, right hand.

DRONE, that long tube belonging to a bagpipe, which, as it sounds only one note, answers as a perpetual bass to the tune.

DRUM, a pulsatile instrument used in military music; it consists of a cylinder, covered at each end by a skin, which may be tightened by means of cords.

——, **KETTLE**. Kettle drums are two large basins of copper with spherical bottoms, and covered at the top with vellum or goat-skin, which is held round the rim by a circle of iron, and tightened or relaxed by screws fixed at the sides for that purpose.

——**MAJOR**, the chief drummer in a regiment.

DUE, (*I.*) two; frequently preceded by *a*; as, *a due*, for two; as,

—— **CORDE**, (*I.*) for two strings.

—— **CORI**, (*I.*) for two choirs or choruses.

DUET, a composition for two voices.

DUETTINO, }
DUETTO, } (*I.*) a short and easy duet.

DUE VOLTE, (*I.*) twice.

DULCIANA, (*I.*) an organ stop, very soft and sweet.

DULCINO, a small bassoon, at one time much used in playing tenor parts to the hautboy.

DULCIMER, a triangular chest strung with wires, which are struck with a little rod held in each hand.

DUMB SPINET, an instrument employed for the purpose of deadening the sound.

DUO, (*I.*) a composition for two voices or instruments.

DUOLO, *con*, (*I.*) with pathos.

DUPLA, double.

DUR, (*G.*) major, in relation to keys and modes; as, *C dur*, C major.

DURATE, }
DURAMENTE, } (*I.*) harshly, coarsely.
DURO, }

DURCHFÜHRUNG, (*G.*) development.

DURCHGEHEND, (*G.*) transient, passing.

DURÉE, (*F.*) length or duration of notes.

DUREZZA, (*I.*) harshness.

DURUM, (*Gk.*) one of the tetrachords in the Guidonian scale.

DUTCH CONCERT, a term of ridicule, and applied to cases where each musician plays his own tune, or in his own time.
DUX, (*L.*) the subject of a fugue.
DYNAMICS, the various degrees of sound.

E.

E, ED, } the Italian conjunction *and*; as, *flauto e violino*, flute and violin; *nobilmente ed animato*, with grandeur and spirit.
ECCEDENTE, (*I.*) augmented, with regard to intervals.
ECCLESIASTICAL MODES. See *Church Modes*.
ECCHUS, an echo of the voice.
ECCO, (*I.*) ECHO, (*F.*) ECO, (*I.*) } a repetition or imitation of a previous passage, with some remarkable modification in regard to tone. This term is often found in organ music.
ECHELLE, (*F.*) the scale or gamut.
ECHEIA, harmonic vases used by the Grecks and Romans in their theatres, for the purpose of augmenting the sound of the voices of the actors.
ECHOMETRE, (*Gk.*) a scale for measuring the duration of sounds.
ECLISSES, (*F. Pl.*) the sides or hoops of a violin, &c.
ECOLE, (*F.*) a school or course of instruction.
ECOSSAIS, ECOSSAISE, } (*F.*) a dance, tune, or air, in the Scotch style.
ECOI, (*Gk.*) tropes or modes sung in the Greek church during Passion-week.
E DUR, (*G.*) E major.
EGLISE, (*F.*) church; as, *musique d'église*, church music.
EGUALE, EGUALIANZA, *con*, EGUALMENTE, } (*I.*) equably, smoothly.
EIGHTH NOTE, a quaver.
EINFACH, (*G.*) simple.
EINGANG, (*G.*) an introduction.
EINHEIT, (*G.*) unity.
EINLEITUNG, (*G.*) an introduction.
EINLEITUNGSSATZ, (*G.*) an introductory movement.
EINSCHNITT, (*G.*) a phrase or imperfect musical sentence.

EIS, (*G.*) E sharp.

EISTEDDVOD, (*Welsh,*) an assemblage of bards.

ELEGAMENTE, ELEGANTE, } (*I.*) with elegance.

ELEGANZA, *con,* (*I.*) with elegance, gracefully.

ELEGIA, an elegy.

ELEGIAC, the style of an elegy.

ELEVAMENTO, ELEVATEZZA, in an elevated style.

ELEVAZIONE, an exalted style.

ELÈVE, (*F.*) a pupil.

ELLINE, (*Gk.*) song of the weavers.

EMBOUCHURE, (*F.*) the mouthpiece of a flute, hautboy, or other wind instrument.

E MOLL, (*G.*) E minor.

EMPFINDUNG, (*G.*) emotion, passion.

EMPHYSOOMENA, instruments designed to imitate the human voice.

EMPHASIS, a particular stress or marked accent on any note.

ENCORE, (*F.*) an expression employed by the audience, at theatres and concerts, to signify their desire that a song or other composition should be repeated.

ENERGICO, CON ENERGIA, or ENERGICAMENTE, (*I.*) with energy.

ENFLER, (*F.*) to increase the tone.

ENGE, (*G.*) close, condensed.

ENHARMONIC, one of the ancient genera; a scale which proceeds by quarter tones.

ENHARMONIQUE, (*F.*) enharmonic.

EN RONDEAU, (*F.*) in imitation of a rondeau.

ENSEIGNEMENT, (*F.*) instruction.

ENSEIGNER, (*F.*) to instruct.

ENSEMBLE, (*F.*) a term applied to music in parts, when the several performers appear to be so animated by one and the same feeling, that the whole is given with that perfect smoothness, both as regards time and style, as to leave nothing further to be desired.

ENTR'ACTE, (*F.*) music played between the acts of the drama.

ENTRATA, (*I.*) an introduction.

ENTUSIASMO, *con,* (*I.*) with enthusiasm.

ENTWURF, (*G.*) sketch or rough draught of a composition.

ENTRE-METS, (*F.*) movements introduced for the sake of variety

ENTREMÉS, (*S.*) a short musical interlude.

ENTRIES, operatic scenes.

ENVOYS, one of the names by which the old English ballads were known.

EOLIAN, the name of one of the ancient modes.

EPI, (*Gk.*) below.

EPICEDIUM, (*Gk.*) a funeral song, or dirge.

EPINETTE, (*F.*) a spinet, an old keyed instrument.

EPISODE, a portion of a composition not founded on the principal subject.

EPITHALAMIUM, (*Gk.*) a nuptial song or ode.

EPIAULA, (*Gk.*) song of the millers.

EPIGONIUM, an instrument having forty strings, so named from Epigonius, its inventor.

EPILENIA, (*Gk.*) song of the grape gatherers.

EPISYNAPHE, when three tetrachords or fourths are sung one after another.

EPINICION, song of triumph.

EPODE, conclusion of a chorus; also, a short lyric poem.

E POI, (*I.*) and then; as, *e poi la coda*, and then the coda.

EPTACHORDO; the same as seventh.

EQUAL VOICES. Compositions for equal voices are those in which either all male or all female voices are employed.

EQUISONANT, of the same or like sound, a unison. This term is often used in guitar playing, to express the different ways of stopping the same note.

EQUISONANCE, (*Gk.*) the consonance of the octave and double octave.

EQUIVOCAL, a term applied to such chords as, by a mere change in the notation, may belong to several keys.

——— **CHORD**, that chord whose fundamental base is not indicated by the interval by which it is formed.

ERHÖHUNG, (*G.*) the raising the pitch of a note by a sharp.

ERNIEDRIGUNG, (*G.*) the depression of a note by means of a flat.

EROTIC, amatory.

EROICO, a symphony in the heroic style.

ERWEITERT, (*G.*) expanded, extended.

ES, (*G.*) E flat.

ESCLAMANDO, operatic scenes in which very loud exclamations occur.

ES DUR, (*G.*) E flat major.

ESES, (*G.*) E double flat.

ES MOLL, (*G.*) E flat minor.

ESSAI, (*F.*) an essay.

ESECUZIONE, (*I.*) execution, great facility in the performance of music, whether vocal or instrumental.

ESERCIZI, (*I.*) exercises, studies for the acquirement of execution.

ESEGUIRE, (*I.*) to execute.

ESPACE, (*F.*) a space, the interval between two lines of the stave.

ESPAGNUOLO, (*I.*) in the Spanish style.

ESPRESSIVO, or CON ESPRESSIONE, (*I.*) with expression.

ESSEMPIO, (*I.*) an example.

ESSENTIAL, a term used to signify those notes of a chord which constitute its real component parts, in contradistinction to all merely accidental or ornamental notes.

ESSACHORDO, the greater and lesser sixth.

ESTRO, (*I.*) elegance and grace.

ESTRINIENDA, a close, confined style of performance.

ESTINGUENDO, (*I.*) diminishing the intensity of the tone by degrees.

ESTINTE, ESTINTO, (*I.*) diminishing, gradually dying away, both as to tone and movement.

ESTRAVAGANZA, (*I.*) a composition or performance characterized by its extravagance or wildness.

ESTREMEMENTE, (*I.*) extremely.

ESTRIBILHO, a favorite Portuguese song in $\frac{6}{8}$ time.

ET, (*L.*) and.

ET INCARNATUS EST, (*L.*) a portion of the Credo.

ETOUFFE, (*F.*) stifled, damped, in harp playing.

ET RESURREXIT, (*L.*) part of the Credo.

ETRUSCAN, (*Gk.*) the music of Etruria, a town whose people were noted for their musical talent.

ETUDE, (*F.*) a study.

ET VITA A (*L.*) a part of the Credo.

EUHARMONIC, in the best concord.

EUPHONIOUS, smooth and melodious.

EUPHONY, sweetness.

EUTHIA, (*Gk.*) a continuity of notes from grave to acute.

EVIRATI, (*I.*) male vocal performers, capable of singing soprano.

EVOLUTIO, (*L.*) inversion.

EXECUTER, (*F.*) to execute or perform either vocally or on an instrument.

EXEQUIÆ, funeral melodies.

EXPRESSION. A performer is said to play with expression when he carefully observes the various modifications of *forte* and *piano*, *legato* and *staccato*, &c., and when, in addition to the above, he imparts to the composition which he is performing a particular charm arising from the impulse of his own feelings.

EXTREMES, those parts of a composition which are the greatest distance from each other in point of gravity or acuteness.

EXTREME, a term relating to intervals in an augmented state. By some authors it is used in conjunction with the word *sharp* or *flat*; extreme sharp answering to *augmented*, and extreme flat to *diminished*.

EXTEMPORE, (*L.*) unpremeditated, extemporaneous.

EXTEMPORIZE, to perform unpremeditatedly.

EXTENDED HARMONY. See *Dispersed Harmony*.

EXTRANEOUS, foreign, far-fetched.

——————— MODULATION, a modulation into some other than the original key and its relatives.

EXTRAVAGANZA, a performance without any regard to rules or good taste.

F.

FA, a syllable applied, in solfaing, to the note F.

FA LA, the burden or chorus of many old English songs.

FA BURDEN, / FALSO BORDONE, (*I.*) / FAUX BOURDON, (*F.*) } a term applied to several ancient species of counterpoint. With regard to modern times, it usually signifies a succession of chords of the sixth, where the interval of the sixth is formed by the extreme parts, and that of the third by the inner part.

FACILITA, (*I.*) facility. This term is generally placed over a passage in small notes intended to facilitate any difficulty.

FACILMENTE, (*I.*) with facility, in an easy manner.

FAGOTTO, (*I.*) a bassoon.

FAGOTTISTA, (*I.*) a performer on the bassoon.

FAGOTTONE, (*I.*) a double bassoon.

FALSE. Those intonations of the voice which do not truly express the intended intervals, as well as all ill-adjusted combinations, and those strings, pipes, and other sonorous bodies which cannot be accurately tuned, are denominated *false*.

——— CADENCE, an imperfect or interrupted cadence.

——— FIFTH, an imperfect or diminished fifth.

——— RELATION, certain harmonic progressions in which notes which have occurred in one chord occur again in the next, altered by means of a sharp, flat, or natural, but not in the very same part, in contradiction to the laws of harmony.

FALSO BORDONE, a term applied in the early days of descant to such counterpoint as had either a drone base, or some part constantly moving in the interval with it.

FALSETTO, (*I.*) certain notes of a man's voice which are above its natural compass, and which can only be produced artificially.

FANCIES, little, lively airs.

FANDANGO, an expressive Spanish dance in $\frac{3}{4}$ time, generally accompanied with castanets.

FANFARE, (*F.*) a trumpet tune.

FANTASIE, (*F.*) } a composition in which the author gives himself
FANTASIA, (*I.*) } up wholly to the caprice of his ideas.

FANTASTICAMENTE, FANTASTICO, (*I.*) expressive of fantastic effects.

FANTASTIQUE, (*F.*) whimsical, fantastical, in relation to style, form, modulation, &c.

FARANDOULE, the name of a lively French dance in $\frac{6}{8}$ time.

FARSA IN MUSICA, a farce or short comic drama set to music, generally in one act.

FASCIE, (*I. Pl.*) the sides of a violin, tenor, or other similar instrument.

FASTOSO, (*I.*) with a lofty and splendid style of execution.

F DUR, (*G.*) the key of F major.

FENIO, I beat, I strike.

FERMO, (*I.*) firm, resolute.

FERMATA, (*I.*) a pause.

FERMAMENTE, FERMATO, } (*I.*) with firmness and decision.

FEROCE, FEROCITA, *con*, } (*I.*) fiercely, with an expression of ferocity.

FES, (*G.*) F flat.

FESCENNINA, the name given to nuptial songs, because they originated with the people of Fescennia, a city of Etruria.

FIACCO, (*I.*) weak, feeble.

FIASCO, (*I.*) a failure.

FIATO, (*I.*) the breath.

FIDICINAL, of the violin species.

FIERAMENTE, FIERO, } (*I.*) in a bold and energetic manner, with vehemence.

FIFRE, (*F.*) FIFFANIO, (*I.*) } a fife.

FIFTEENTH, an organ stop, tuned two octaves above the diapasons; also an interval of two octaves.

FIGURATO, (*I.*) FIGURÉ, (*F.*) } figured; as, *basso figurato*, a figured bass.

FIGURED BASS, a bass having figures placed over the notes to indicate the harmony.

FILAR LA VOCE, (*I.*) to gradually augment and diminish the sound of the voice.

FILUM, (*L.*) former name of the stem of a note.

FIN, (*F.*) FINE, (*I.*) } the end. This expression is generally used to indicate the termination of a musical composition.

FINALE, the last piece of any act of an opera, or of a concert; or the last movement of a symphony or sonata, in the German style.

FINGERSATZ, (*G.*) fingering.

FINITO, (*I.*) concluded, terminated.

FINGER-BOARD, that part of a stringed instrument on which the fingers press.

FINGERED, that tone caused by the pressure of the fingers.

FIN QUI, (*I.*) to this place.

FINTO, (*I.*) feigned; or, with regard to cadences, interrupted.

FIORITURE, (*I.*) embellishments in singing; divisions of rapid notes.

FIOREGGIANTE, (*I.*) decorated with flourishes.
FIORISCENTE, (*I.*) an ornamental style.
FIORITO, (*I.*) embellishments.
FIORITTO, a species of diminution, commonly made at the ending of a cadence.
FIS, (*G.*) F sharp.
FIS DUR, (*G.*) F sharp major.
FISFIS, (*G.*) F double sharp.
FIS MOLL, (*G.*) F sharp minor.
FISTULA, (*L.*) a pipe, or flute in general.
——— DULCIS, (*L.*) a common flute.
——— GERMANICA, (*L.*) German flute.
——— PANIS, (*L.*) an instrument formed of reeds.
——— PASTORALIS, (*L.*) shepherd's pipe.
——— PASTORICA, (*L.*) the name given by Cicero and other classics to the oaten pipe, used by the audiences at Roman theatres in expression of disapprobation.
FITHELE, ancient name of the violin.
FLAUTATO, FLAUTANDO, (*I.*) with a flute-like tone. This term is sometimes met with in violin music, and the desired quality of tone is obtained by drawing the bow smoothly and gently across the strings, over that end of the finger-board nearest the bridge.
FLAUTINO, FLAUTONE, (*I.*) an octave flute.
FLAUTISTA, (*I.*) a performer on the flute.
FLAUTO, (*I.*) a flute.
——— PICCOLO, (*I.*) an octave flute, or a flageolet.
——— TRAVERSO, (*I.*) the German flute.
FLEBILE, (*I.*) in a mournful style.
FLEBILMENTE, (*I.*) mournful.
F-LÖCHER, (*G. Pl.*) the sound holes of a violin, tenor, &c.
FLON-FLON, the burden of certain old vaudevilles. The term is now applied in contempt to any air resembling them in style.
FLOURISH, an appellation sometimes given to decorative notes which a singer or instrumental performer adds to a passage, with the double view of heightening the effect of the piece, and of displaying his own flexibility of voice or finger.
FLORID, ornamental, figured, embellished.
——— SONG, applied by musicians of the fourteenth century

to the invention of *figured descant*, to distinguish it from the old chant, or plain song.

FLUGEL, (*G.*) a harpsichord.

FLUTE, a portable, inflatile instrument, blown with the breath, and consisting of a boxen or ivory tube, furnished with holes at the side for the purpose of varying its sounds. Its name is derived from the word *fluta*, the Latin name of the lamprey, or small eel, taken in the Sicilian seas; because, like that fish, it is long, and perforated at the side. The flute was in great esteem with the ancient Greeks and Romans.

FLUTE-A-BEC, (*F.*) an English flute.

FLUTA, (*L.*) flute.

FLUTED, a term applied to those upper and extra notes of a soprano voice, which, from the constraint with which they are produced, are thin, and of a flute-like tone.

FLUTE ALLEMANDE, }
——— TRAVERSIERE, } (*F.*) the German flute.

F MOLL, (*G.*) the key of F minor.

FOCOSO, (*I.*) with fire.

FOGLIETTO, (*I.*) a continuation of the violin.

FOLLIA, (*S.*) a Spanish air, or dance tune, so called.

——— DI SPAGNA, (*S.*) a species of composition, consisting of variations on a given air, invented by the Spaniards; hence its name.

FONDAMENTO, (*I.*) the base.

FORTE, (*I.*) FOR., *abb.*, loud.

FORLANA, (*I.*) }
FORLANE, (*F.*) } a lively Venetian dance in $\frac{6}{8}$ time.

FORTEMENT, (*F.*) loudly, with force.

FORTE-PIANO, (*I.*) the piano is so called by reason of its capability of modifying the intensity of the sounds.

FORTISSIMO, (*I.*) very loud.

FORTSETZUNG, (*G.*) a continuation.

FORZANDO, (*I.*) FORZ., *abb.* This term implies that the note is to be marked with particular emphasis or force.

FORZA, FORZATO, (*I.*) force; as, *con forza*, with force, vehemently.

FORMULARY, name formerly given to the stated and prescribed number and disposition of the ecclesiastical tones.

FORAMINA, (*L.*) flute holes.

FOURTEENTH, an interval of an octave and a seventh.

FOURTH, an interval of four degrees.

F QUADRATA, the name given by the early writers on counterpoint to the sign which represented sharp F, in their *musica falsa* or transpositions, and the form of which, like our naturals, approached that of a square.

FRANCHEZZA, *con*, (*I.*) with freedom, boldly.

FRASI, (*I. Pl.*) phrases, short musical sentences.

FREDDAMENTE, FREDDEZZA, *con*, (*I.*) coldly, with coldness.

FREDON, (*F.*) a flourish, or other extemporaneous embellishment.

FRENCH SIXTH, the name of a chord composed of a major third, extreme fourth, and extreme sixth; as, F ♯, D, C, A ♭.

——— HORN, the *corne de chasse*, a wind instrument, consisting of a long tube twisted into several circular folds, and gradually increasing in diameter from the end at which it is blown to that at which the sound issues.

FRESCO, FRESCAMENTE, new or uncommon.

FRETS, those small projections fixed across the finger-board of a guitar, mandoline, and other instruments, to show where the notes are to be stopped.

FRETTA, or *con* FRETTA, quickening or hastening the time.

FREY, (*G.*) free; as, *freye schreibart*, the free style of composition.

FROSCH, (*G.*) the nut of a bow for the violin, tenor, &c.

F SCHLÜSSEL, (*G.*) the F clef.

FUGA, (*I.*) a fugue; a subject treated in imitation, or a dialogue, in which the different parts pursue each other alternately.

FUGATO, (*I.*) a piece in the fugue style.

FUGHETTA, (*I.*) a short fugue.

FUGA DOPPIA, a fugue with two subjects.

FUGUE, a form of composition peculiar to the strict or contrapunctal style, in which a subject is proposed by one part, and then answered by other parts, according to certain rules.

FUGUIST, a composer or performer of fugues.

FUGUE RENVERSEE, (*F.*) a fugue, the answer of which is made in contrary motion to that of the subject.

FÜHRER, (*G.*) the subject of a fugue.

FULL, for all the voices or instruments. In cathedral music, it implies that the passage is to be sung by both sides of the choir.

FULL ORGAN, an organ fully employed, all its stops required.
——— TURN, a turn consisting of four notes immediately after that upon which it is made.
——— ANTHEM, an anthem in four or more parts, without verses; to be sung in chorus.
——— SCORE, a complete score of all the parts of a complete composition, whether vocal or instrumental, or both combined.
——— SERVICE, a service without any verse parts.
FUNDAMENTAL BASS, a bass formed of the roots of chords only. A bass of this sort is not meant to be played, but merely to serve as a test of the correct progression of the harmony.
——————— CHORD, a chord the lowest note of which is its root.
FUNEBRE, (*F.* and *I.*) } funeral; as, *marche funèbre*, a funeral
FUNEREO, (*I.*) } march.
FUNZIONI, (*I. Pl.*) sacred musical performances in general, as oratorios, masses, &c.
FUOCO, *con*, (*I.*) with fire, with intense animation.
FUOCOSO, (*I.*) extremely spirited.
FURIA, *con*, FURIBONDO, FURIOSAMENTE, FURIOSO, (*I.*) with extreme vehemence, furiously.
FURLANO, (*I.*) an antiquated dance.
FURNITURE, an organ stop, consisting of several ranks of pipes.
FURORE, *con*, (*I.*) with fury, with great agitation.
FURCE, name formerly given to a close diatonic chain of ascending and descending notes, introduced to connect an expansive interval.
FUSA, (*L.*) a quaver.
FUSELLA, (*L.*) the name formerly applied to the demisemiquaver.

G.

GAIAMENT, (*I.*) } in a cheerful and lively style.
GAIEMENTE, (*F.*) }
GAI, (*F.*) }
GAIO, (*I.*) } gayly, cheerfully.
GAJO, (*I.*) }
GAGLIARDA, (*I.*) }
GAILLARDE, (*F.*) } a lively dance tune, in triple time.
GALLIARD, }

GALANTEMENTE, (*I.*) gallantly, boldly.

GALLOPADE, (*F.*) a galop, a quick German dance tune.

GALOP, (*G.*) }
GALOPPE, (*F.*) } a quick species of dance, generally in $\frac{2}{4}$ time.

GAMME, (*F.*) the scale of any key.

GAMUT, the scale of notes belonging to any key.

GANZE, (*G.*) whole; as, *ganze note*, a whole note or semibreve; *ganzeton*, a whole tone.

GARBO, (*I.*) with simplicity, without pretension, unaffectedly.

GARRIRE, (*I.*) to warble like a bird.

GAUCHE, (*F.*) left; as, *main gauche*, left hand.

GAVOT, a lively dance in common time.

GAVOTTA, (*I.*) a gavot, a lively species of dance.

G DUR, (*G.*) the key of G major.

GEBROCHENE AWKORDE, (*G. Pl.*) broken chords, arpeggios.

GEBUNDEN, (*G.*) connected, syncopated, in regard to the style of playing or writing.

GEDACHT, (*G.*) stopped, in opposition to the open pipes in an organ.

GEFÄHRTE, (*G.*) the answer of a fugue.

GEFÜHE, *mit*, (*G.*) with feeling and sentiment.

GEGENBEWEGUNG, (*G.*) contrary motion.

GEHEND, (*G.*) This word signifies a degree of movement similar to that implied by *andante*.

GEIGE, (*G.*) the violin.

GENUS, GENERA, (*L.*) terms used by the ancients to indicate the modes according to which they divided their tetrachords, whether by tones and semitones conjointly, by semitones only, or by the occasional intervention of quarter tones. The first mode was called the diatonic genus, the second the chromatic genus, and the third the enharmonic genus.

——— **MELODIÆ**, (*L.*) the manner in which the ancients divided and subdivided the elements of melody.

——— **MODULANDI**, (*L.*) the ancient division of the tetrachord; a disposition of its four sounds in succession.

GENERATORE, (*F.*) that tone which generates. Name given by Rameau to the fundamental note of the common chord.

GENERALBASS, (*G.*) thorough-bass.

GENERATING TONE, the principal tone caused by the vibration of stringed instruments when one tone is struck.

GENIALIA, musical instruments used by the Romans in celebrating nuptial ceremonies.

GENEROSO, (*I.*) nobly, in a dignified manner.

GENRE, (*F.*) style; also, genus; as,

——— CHROMATIQUE, (*F.*) the chromatic genus.

GENTILEZZA, *con*, (*I.*) with grace and elegance.

GERADE BEWEGUNG, (*G.*) similar motion.

——— TAKTART, (*G.*) common time.

GERMAN SIXTH, the name applied by some writers to a chord composed of a major third, perfect fifth, and extreme sixth; as, A #, G, E, C.

——— FLUTE, a German invention, blown at the side instead of end, as is the English.

GES, (*G.*) G flat.

GESANG, (*G.*) singing, or the art of singing; also, a song.

GESCHWIND, (*G.*) quick; as,

——— MARSCH, (*G.*) a quick march.

GES DUR, (*G.*) the key of G flat major.

GESTOURS, (*F.*) itinerant minstrels of the humorous order, who interlarded their songs with comic tales and jokes.

GIGA, (*I.*)
GIGUE, (*F.*) } a jig, or lively species of dance.

G IN ALT, the first note in *alt*.

——— ALTISSIMO, the first note in *altissimo*.

GIOCOSAMENTE, GIOCOSO, (*I.*) humorously, with sportiveness.

GIOJOSO, (*I.*) joyously, with buoyant hilarity.

GIOVALE, (*I.*) jovially.

GIS, (*G.*) G sharp.

——— MOLL, (*G.*) the key of G sharp minor.

G MOLL, (*G.*) the key of G minor.

G SCHLÜSSEL, (*G.*) G clef.

GIUOCO, (*I.*) a stop of an organ.

GIUSTAMENTE, (*I.*) justly, with precision.

GIUSTO, (*I.*) in just and exact time.

GIULLARI, or GIOCOLARI, bands of buffoons, dancers, actors, singers, and instrumental performers, retained in courts of princes in Tuscany, for the diversion of the company.

GLEE, a composition for three or more voices, generally in a cheerful style.

GLI, (*I. Pl.*) the; as, *gli stromenti*, the instruments.

GLIDING, an easy, smooth, and graceful style.

GLISSER, (*F.*) to glide smoothly from one key to another.

GLISSANDO, (*I.*) in a gliding manner.

GLISSICATO, (*I.*) in a gentle and gliding manner.

GLORIA, (*L.*) a principal movement of the mass or Catholic service.

GLORIFICATION, vocal praise.

GLOTTIS, (*Gk.*) the mouthpiece of all wind instruments.

GLOTTOCOMEIA, (*G.*) boxes in which the Greeks carried the *lingulæ*, or tongues of their flutes.

GNACCARE, castanets.

GOL, a funeral dirge of the Irish peasantry.

GONG, an instrument supposed to be of Chinese origin, which consists of a large round plate of bell metal, which, when struck, produces a loud noise.

GORGHEGGI, (*I. Pl.*) vocal exercises for acquiring facility in the execution of divisions.

GRACES, ornamental notes, sometimes indicated by the composer, sometimes added spontaneously by the performer. The most usual are the appoggiatura, the turn, and the shake.

GRADAZIONE, *con Gradazione*, (*I.*) expresses the gradual augmentation or diminution of celerity of movement or intensity of tone.

GRADO, (*I.*) a degree or single step on the stave.

GRADUALE, the Gradual; a verse sung after the epistle in Catholic churches.

GRADUELLEMENT, (*F.*) gradually.

GRADUAL MODULATION, modulation in which, before the modulating chord, some chord is taken which may be considered as belonging either to the key we are in, or that to which we are going.

GRAN, (*I.*) grand.

——— **GUSTO**, (*I.*) in a lofty, elevated manner.

GRANDE, (*I.*) great; as, *con grande espressione*, with much expression.

GRAND MESURE A DEUX TEMS, (*F.*) ₵ time.

GRAND CANTORE, (*I.*) a vocalist of uncommon merit.

——— CASSA, the double drum.

GRANDIOSO, (*I.*) in a noble and elevated style.

GRAPPA, (*I.*) the brace or character serving to connect two or more staves.

GRATIAS AGIMUS, (*L.*) part of the Gloria.

GRAVEMENTE, (*I.*) with gravity, dignified and solemn.

GRAVE, (*I.*) a very slow and solemn movement; also, a deep, low pitch in the scale of sounds.

GRAVEZZA, grave.

GRAVITA, *con*, (*I.*) with gravity.

GRAVITY, a low pitch.

GRAZIA, *con*, GRAZIOSAMENTE, GRAZIOSO, (*I.*) in a flowing and graceful style.

GREAT CADENCE, a cadence in which the closing chord immediately follows that of the sub-dominant.

——— ORGAN. In an organ with three rows of keys, this is usually the middle row; it is so called from containing the greatest number of stops, as also from the pipes being voiced louder than those in the swell or the choir organ.

GREGORIANISCHE GESANG, (*G.*) the Gregorian chant.

GREGORIAN MUSIC, sacred compositions introduced into the Catholic service by Pope Gregory.

GREGORIAN TONES. This term sometimes refers to the chants used for the psalms in the Roman Catholic service, and at others to the ancient modes or tones on which those chants are based. See *Church Modes*.

GRIFFBRET, (*G.*) the finger-board of a violin, violoncello, &c.

GROS-FA, the name formerly applied to old church music in square notes, semibreves, and minims.

——— TAMBOUR, (*F.*) the great drum.

GROSSE, (*G.*) major, in regard to intervals.

——— CAISSE, (*F.*) the great drum.

——— SONATE, (*G. Pl.*) grand sonatas.

GROSSO, (*I.*) full, great; as, *concerto grosso*, a concerto for many instruments.

GROTTESCO, unique, grotesque.

GROUND, a bass, consisting of a few simple notes, intended as a theme on which, at each repetition, a new melody is constructed.

GROUP, an assemblage of several short notes tied together.

GRUNDSTIMME, (*G.*) the bass.

GRUNDTON, (*G.*) the bass note.

GRUPPETTO, (*I.*) a group of notes, a turn.

GRUPPO, (*I.*) a turn, or grace.

GUARACHA, a Spanish dance.

GUDDOK, a rustic violin, with three strings, used among the Russian peasantry.

GUERRIERO, (*I.*) in a martial style.

GUIDA, (*I.*) a guide; as, *guida armonica*, a guide to harmony.

GUIDA, (*I.*) } the character called a "direct."
GUIDON, (*F.*) }

GUIDONIAN SYLLABLES. See *Aretinian Syllables.*

GUIDA MUSICA, a guide to musical knowledge.

GUITAR, a well-known stringed instrument, the body of which is of an oval form, and the neck similar to that of a violin.

GUIDE, a name given to that note in a fugue which leads off and announces the subject.

GUSTO, GUSTOSO, or CON GUSTO, (*I.*) with taste, elegantly.

GUTTURAL, formed too much in the throat.

GYMNASTICE, (*Gk.*) contests of skill among the ancients, in which the performance of music formed a principal part.

H.

H. This letter is used by the Germans for B natural.

HABITUDO, a ratio measuring an interval.

HACKBRETT, (*G.*) the dulcimer.

HALBERTON, (*G.*) a semitone.

HALBCADENZ, (*G.*) a half cadence; a cadence on the dominant.

HALBNOTE, (*G.*) } a minim. 𝅗𝅥
HALF-NOTE, }

——CIRCLE, a melodic figure consisting of four tones, the second and fourth of which are the same.

HALLELUJAH, a Hebrew word signifying "Praise the Lord."

HALS, (*G.*) the neck of a violin, tenor, &c.

HAND-GUIDE, an instrument invented by Kalkbrenner, to insure a good position of the hands and arms on the piano-forte.

HARDIMENT, (*F.*) with boldness and animation.

HARFE, (*G.*) a harp.

HARMONIPHON, a little instrument, with a key-board like a piano-forte, invented in 1837, and intended to supply the place of the hautboys in the orchestra. The sounds are produced from small metal tongues, acted upon by blowing through a flexible tube.

HARMONICA, a musical instrument, the tones of which are produced from globular glasses.

HARMONICI, (*I. Pl.*) harmonics in violin music.

HARMONIE, (*F.* and *G.*) harmony in general; also, music expressly composed for a military band.

HARMONY, the art of combining notes so as to form chords, and of causing the chords thus formed to succeed each other according to certain laws.

HARMONICS, certain indistinct sounds, which, by attentively listening to the vibrations of any deep-toned musical string, may be heard to accompany the principal sound. *Harmonics* are also certain artificial notes produced from the violin, violoncello, harp, &c., and which somewhat resemble the tones of a flageolet.

HARMONIST, one acquainted with the laws of harmony.

HARMONIZER, one who fabricates or produces harmony. The term is generally applied to those musicians who add passages to the productions of others, fill up scanty pieces, or garnish popular airs.

HARMONIZED. A melody is said to be harmonized, when additional parts are subjoined, so as to give it body, or a fulness of effect.

HARMONIC HAND, the figure of the left hand, with the syllabic signs of the intervals of the three hexachords, instituted by Guido, marked on the joints of the fingers. In some ancient works it is called the *Guidonian hand.*

———— MODULATION, a change in the harmony from one key to another.

HARMONIOUS, a term applicable to any two or more sounds which form a consonant or agreeable union.

HARMONOMETRE, a string drawn between two points, over bridges so arranged as to be lengthened or shortened at pleasure, and used for measuring the harmonic relations.

HARMATIAN or **CHARIOT AIR,** (*Gk.*) a spirited martial air, employed to animate the horses that drew the chariot during battle.

HARMONICAL SOUNDS, those produced by the parts of the chords, &c., which vibrate a certain number of times, while the whole chord vibrates once.

HARP, a stringed instrument consisting of a triangular frame, having chords distended in parallel directions from the upper part to one of its sides.

HARPER or **HARPIST,** a performer on the harp.

HARP-BELL, a stringed instrument, so called from its being swung about in performance, like a bell. It is about three feet long; its strings, which are of no determinate number, are of brass or steel wire, fixed at one end, and held at the other by screws.

HARP LUTE, an instrument having twelve strings, and resembling the guitar.

HARPALICE, (*Gk.*) a song appropriated to young girls.

HARPEGGIATO, causing several sounds of one accord to be heard, not together, but distinctly one after the other.

HARPSICHORD, an instrument much used before the invention of the piano-forte. Its strings were of wire, and it was furnished with one, and sometimes with two rows of keys.

HART, (*G.*) major, in regard to keys and modes.

HAUPT, (*G.*) principal.

HAUPTMANUAL, (*G.*) the set of keys belonging to the great organ.

HAUPTNOTE, HAUPT-TON, (*G.*) the principal note of a shake, or that over which the mark tr is placed.

HAUPTPERIOD, (*G.*) a capital period.

HAUPTSATZ, (*G.*) the principal subject or theme.

HAUPTSCHLUSS, (*G.*) a final cadence.

HAUPTSTIMME, (*G.*) a principal part.

HAUPTWERK, (*G.*) the great organ.

HAUSSE, (*F.*) the nut of a violin or other bow.

HAUT, (*F.*) acute, high, shrill; as, *haut contre*, high, or counter tenor; *haut dessus*, first treble.

——— **CONTRE,** (*F.*) high, or counter tenor.

——— **DESSUS,** (*F.*) first treble.

H DUR, (*G.*) B major.

HEMI, a word used in connection with some other word, the value of which it diminishes one half.

HEMIDIAPENTE, (*Gk.*) the diminished or imperfect fifth.

HEMITONE, (*Gk.*) an old term signifying the interval of a major third diminished by half a tone.

HEMIOPE, or HEMIOPEUS, (*Gk.*) a wind instrument used by the ancients, consisting of a tube with three holes.

HEMITUONO, (*I.*) a name given by the Italians to one of the intervals of music.

HEPTAMERIS, (*Gk.*) in ancient music, the seventh part of a *meris*, or forty-third part of an octave.

HEPTAPHONOS, one of the ten musical notes of the middle ages.

HEPTACHORD, a scale or system of seven notes.

HERSTRICH or HERABSTRICH, (*G.*) a down bow.

HERALDS, or DES HERAUTS. This appellation the French formerly applied to the minstrels, because, on account of the strength of their voices, they were qualified to animate the soldiers in battle, and to make proclamations at public festivals.

HESYCHIASTIC, (*Gk.*) a chord in ancient music equivalent to a modern sixth.

HEXACHORD, a scale or system of six notes.

HEY-DERRY-DOWN, an old English burden. See *Burden.*

HEY-TROLLY-LOLY, an old Scotch burden. See *Burden.*

HIDDEN CONSECUTIVES, such as occur in passing, by similar motion, from an imperfect to a perfect concord, or from one perfect concord to another of a different kind.

HILARODI, (*Gk.*) strolling musicians, who went about singing diverting songs.

HILARODIA, (*Gk.*) songs and lyric poems sung by the Hilarodi.

HINAUFSTRICH, HINSTRICH, (*G.*) an up bow.

HIS, (*G.*) B sharp.

HISTRIO, (*L.*) a stage singer or mimic.

H MOLL, (*G.*) the key of B minor.

HOCHZEITMARSCH, (*G.*) a nuptial march.

HOCKET, a mode of execution corresponding with that of our staccato passages.

HOLDING-NOTE, a note prolonged during the changes of other notes.

HOMOPHONY, (*Gk.*) a word applied by the ancients to that kind of music which was performed in unison.

HOMOPHONOI, (*Gk.*) duplicates of the same sound.

HOMOPHONOUS, voices in unison.

HOPSWALZER, (*G.*) quick waltzes.

HORNPIPE, the name of an old dance in triple time. Modern tunes of this name are usually in common time.

HOSANNA, (*L.*) part of the Sanctus.

HÜLFSNOTE, HÜLFSTON, (*G.*) the auxiliary note of a shake.

HUNTING MUSIC, music designed for a hunting tour.

HURDY-GURDY, an instrument, the strings of which are caused to vibrate by the friction of a wheel upon them.

HURTIG, (*G.*) quick, implying a degree of movement similar to that indicated by the word *allegro.*

HYDRAULICA, an ancient instrument whose tones were produced by the motion of water.

HYMEE, (*Gk.*) song of the millers.

HYMENÆA, (*Gk.*) a marriage song used by the Greeks.

HYMN, anciently a song in honor of the gods or of heroes. It is the oldest of poetical compositions, and was thought by the ancients to be dictated by the gods. In the present acceptation of the word, it signifies a short, religious, lyric poem.

HYPATE, (*Gk.*) the lowest of the tetrachords.

——— **BAREIA GRAVIS,** (*Gk.*) a tone in ancient music produced by eight ninths of the whole string.

——— **DIATONUS,** (*Gk.*) the third sound of the first tetrachord.

———**HYPATON,** (*Gk.*) the lowest chord of the lowest tetrachord.

——— **MESON,** (*Gk.*) the last or highest of the first tetrachord, and the first or lowest of the second tetrachord.

HYPATOIDES, (*Gk.*) the deep or bass sounds.

HYPER, (*Gk.*) above.

———**ÆOLIAN,** (*Gk.*) name given by the ancients to their penultima mode upward, the fundamental or tonic of which was a fourth above that of the Æolian.

———**DIAZEUXIS,** (*Gk.*) a disjunction of two tetrachords when separated by the interval of an octave.

———**DORIAN,** (*Gk.*) a mode among the ancients, said to have been invented by Pythaclydes, the fundamental of which was a fourth above the Dorian.

HYPER-IONIAN, (*Gk.*) one of the ancient modes.

———LYDIAN, (*Gk.*) the highest ancient mode, the fundamental of which was a fourth above that of the Lydian.

———MIXO-LYDIAN, (*Gk.*) one of the ancient Greek modes.

———PHRYGIAN, or HYPER-MIXO-LYDIAN, (*Gk.*) the highest of the thirteen modes of Aristoxenus, forming the diapason, or octave, with the Hypodorian, or lowest mode.

HYPERBOLÆON, or SUPREME, (*Gk.*) the fifth tetrachord, so called because its sounds were more acute than those of the other four.

HYPERIASTIAN, or HYPER-IONIAN, (*Gk.*) the general name of an ancient mode which had its fundamental a fourth above that of the Ionian.

HYPEROCHE, (*Gk.*) a word used by ancient authors to signify the difference between the enharmonic and chromatic dieses.

HYPO, (*Gk.*) below.

———ÆOLIAN, a mode having its fundamental a fourth below that of the Æolian.

———DIAZEUXIS, (*Gk.*) the interval of a fifth, found between two tetrachords separated disjunctively.

———DORIAN, (*Gk.*) the lowest of the Greek modes.

———IASTIAN, (*Gk.*) one of the ancient modes.

———IONIAN, (*Gk.*) the second of the ancient modes. Its lowest sound was a fourth below that of the Ionian.

———LYDIAN, (*Gk.*) the fifth of the ancient modes; the fundamental was a fourth below that of the Lydian.

———MIXO-LYDIAN, (*Gk.*) a mode added by Guido to those of the ancient Greeks.

———PHRYGIAN, (*Gk.*) a mode said to have been invented by a pupil of Socrates. Its fundamental was a fourth lower than that of the Phrygian, from which it was derived.

———PROSLAMBANOMENOS, (*Gk.*) a chord added by Guido to the ancient scale. It was a tone lower than the lowest sound of the Greeks.

———SYNAPHE, (*Gk.*) a term applied by the ancients to the disjunction of two tetrachords by the interposition of a third, conjoint with both.

HYPOCHERMES, (*Gk.*) a canticle or song used by the ancients in their military dances, and feasts of the gods.

HYPOCRITIC, (*Gk.*) an epithet applied by the ancients to the art of gesticulation, which had a considerable share in their public vocal performances.

I.

IAMBUS, a musical foot, consisting of one short and one long note.

IAMBICS, certain songs or satires which are supposed to have given birth to the ancient comedy. There were two kinds; one for singing, the other for recitation.

IASTIAN, the name of one of the ancient modes.

IL, (*I.*) the; as, *il violino*, the violin.

— CANTO, (*I.*) the song.

— PIU, (*I.*) the most.

— PONTICELLO, (*I.*) that precise part of the voice where the natural tone forms a juncture with the falsetto. It also denotes that in violin playing the bow must be carried near the bridge.

— PASSO TEMPO, (*I.*) a short composition intended as a diversion.

— SDRUCCIOLARE, (*I.*) a sliding movement over the keys of a piano.

— TEMPO CRESCENDO, accelerating the time.

— VOLTEGGIARE, (*I.*) crossing the hands in piano music.

IMBOCCATURA, (*I.*) the mouthpiece of a wind instrument.

IMBROGLIO, a confusion, caused by the complication of the various parts.

IMITANDO, (*I.*) imitating; as, *imitando la voce*, imitating the inflections of the voice.

IMITATIVE, a term applicable to that music which is composed in imitation of the effects of some of the operations of nature, art, or human passion.

IMITAZZIONE, a particular style of composition, wherein each part is made to imitate the other.

IMMEDIATE CADENCE, common cadence.

IMPAZIENTEMENTE, (*I.*) with impatience.

IMPERFECT, less than perfect, or minor, in speaking of intervals, chords, &c.

IMPERFECT CADENCE, a cadence in which the dominant harmony is preceded by the common chord of the tonic.

——— CONSONANCES, a term applied, in harmony, to the major and minor thirds, and major and minor sixths.

——— CONCORD. This term is applied to concords, except the fourth and fifth.

——— MEASURE, the name by which twofold measure was once designated.

——— PERIOD, a termination that does not fully satisfy the ear.

IMPERFETTO, imperfect.

IMPERIOSO, authoritative, imperative.

IMPETO, *con*, IMPETUOSITA, *con*, IMPETUOSO, IMPETUOSAMENTE, (*I.*) with impetuosity.

IMPONENTE, (*I.*) with haughtiness.

IMPRESSARIO, (*I.*) the name given to the manager of an opera.

IMPROMPTU, (*F.*) an extemporaneous production.

IMPROVVISAMENTE, (*I.*) extemporaneously.

IMPROVVISARE, (*I.*) to compose or sing extemporaneously.

IMPROVVISATORI, (*I. Pl.*) persons gifted with the power of reciting or singing verses extemporaneously.

IN, (*I.*) in; as, *in tempo*, in time.

— ALT. This term is applied to notes which are situated above F on the top line of the treble stave.

— ALTISSIMO. All notes which run higher than F above the third additional line in the treble are said to be in *altissimo*.

INCISORE DI NOTE, (*I.*) an engraver of music.

INCORDARE, (*I.*) to string an instrument.

INCIDENTAL, airs, duets, trios, &c., called forth by the general tenor of a drama.

INCOMPOSITE, those intervals which are simply constituted, and in the calculation of which we take no notice of the intermediaries, but only consider the terms.

INCONSONANCE, the effect of two discordants, or disagreeing sounds.

INDECISO, (*I.*) undecided. This term indicates slight changes of time, and a somewhat capricious value of the notes.

INDEX. See *Direct.*

INDIFFERENZA, *con,* (*I.*) with indifference, irresolutely.

IN DISPARTE, used in operatic music to signify that the part is to be addressed to some one aside or not taking a part in the performance.

INFANTILE, (*I.*) childlike, infantine; the thin quality of tone observable in the upper notes of some female voices.

INFERNALE, (*I.*) infernal.

INFLATILE. Wind instruments, as flutes, clarinets, &c., are so termed.

INFLECTION, any change or modification in the pitch or tone of the voice.

INFINITE. Those canons are thus called which are so constructed that the end leads to the beginning, and the performance of which may be incessantly repeated.

INFRA, beneath.

IN FUGUE, any movement the chief feature of which is constituted by the support of a single subject.

INGANNO, (*I.*) a deception. It is generally applied to interrupted cadences, though occasionally also to any unusual resolution of a discord, or unexpected modulation.

INNOCENTEMENTE, INNOCENTE, INNOCENZA, *con,* (*I.*) in an artless and simple style.

INNO, (*I.*) a hymn.

IN PALCO, (*I.*) a stage performance. Oratorios were originally performed in Italy on a stage erected in the church; that is, *in palco.*

INQUIETO, (*I.*) perturbed, uneasy, with disquietude.

INSEGNAMENTO, (*I.*) instruction.

INSENSIBILMENTE, (*I.*) insensibly, by small degrees.

INSTRUMENT, in music, any sonorous body artificially constructed for the production of sound. They are divided into three kinds — wind instruments, stringed instruments, and instruments of percussion.

———— A ARCHET, (*F.*) a bow instrument.

———— VENT, (*F.*) a wind instrument.

INSTRUMENTAL MUSIC, music composed for instruments.

INSTRUMENTATION, the finishing of an instrumental piece; the act of embellishing or filling up an outline.

INSTRUMENTAZIONE, (*I.*) a term equivalent to instrumentation, or adaptation for the orchestra.

INTAVOLARE, or INTAVOLATURA, (*I.*) musical notation.

INTENTIO, (*L.*) the passage of the voice from grave to acute.

INTERRUPTED, a term applied to those closes or cadences in which the bass, instead of falling or rising from the fifth to the key-note, passes to some other, and interrupts the full close, or final cadence.

INTERLUDE,
INTERLUDIUM, (*L.*) } an intermediate strain or movement.

INTERMEZZI, (*I. Pl.*) interludes or detached dances introduced between the acts of an opera.

INTERMEZZO, (*I.*) intermediate, placed between two others.

INTERRUZIONE, (*I.*) an interruption; as, *senza interruzione*, play on without interruption.

INTERVAL, the distance, or difference of pitch, between two notes.

INTERVALLE, (*F.*)
INTERVALLO, (*I.*) } an interval.

INTERMEDIATE, a term sometimes applied to accidentals.

IN TRIPOLI, a composition in three parts.

INTRODUCTORY, movements preparative of that which is to follow.

INTRODUTTORIO, (*I.*) introduction.

INTRODUCTION, that movement in a composition designed to bespeak the attention, and prepare the ear for the movements that are to follow.

INTRATTO, a martial air performed at a triumphal entrance of an army or procession.

INTONATION, in singing, implies the emission of the voice so as to produce any required note in proper tune.

INTONATE, to sound the notes.

INTONAZIONE, (*I.*) intonation.

INTRADA, INTRODUCIMENTO, INTRODUZIONE, (*I.*) an introduction.

INTREPIDAMENTE, INTREPIDEZZA, *con*, (*I.*) with intrepidity.

INTROITUS, (*L.*) the beginning of the mass or Catholic service.

INVERSION, such a change of position in respect to intervals and chords as arises from placing the upper notes at bottom, and the bottom notes above.

INVERTED TURN, an embellishment formed by prefixing three notes to a principal note.

INVITATORIUM, (*L.*) a term applied to the antiphone or response to the psalm *Venite, exultemus.*

INVOCAZIONE, (*I.*) an invocation, a prayer.

IO BACCHE, (*L.*) a Bacchanalian burden in the lyric poetry of the Romans.

— **TRIUMPHE**, (*L.*) in the lyric poetry of the Romans, a shout of triumph.

IONIAN, one of the Greek modes.

IRATAMENTE, IRATE, (*I.*) passionately, with anger.

IRLANDAIS, IRLANDAISE, (*F.*) a dance or melody in the Irish style.

IRONICAMENTE, (*I.*) ironically.

IRRESOLUTO, (*I.*) irresolutely, hesitatingly.

IRRELATIVE, a term applied to any two chords which do not contain some sound common to both.

IRREGOLARE, irregular. Modes are thus called when they run many degrees both above and below their octaves. A cadence is said to be irregular when it does not end upon one of the essential chords of the mode in which the piece is composed.

ISOCHRONOUS, (*Gk.*) an equality of time in the various parts.

ISTRONENTE MUSICO, (*I.*) a musical instrument.

ISTESSO, (*I.*) the same; as, *istesso tempo*, the same time.

ITHYMBOS, (*Gk.*) a dance in honor of the Bacchanalian deity of the Greeks.

ITALIENNE, (*F.*) Italian; as, *à l'Italienne*, in the Italian style.

ITALIAN SIXTH, that species of the chord of the superfluous sixth in which that interval is accompanied only by a major third. In the key of G, this chord will run

ITA MISSA EST, (*L.*) the termination of the mass, sung by the priest to Gregorian music.

J.

JAEGER CHOR, (*G.*) hunting chorus.

JALEME, (*Gk.*) a mournful song.

JAR, to disagree in sound.

JARGON, the result of the union of two or more discordant sounds.

JEUX, (*F. Pl.*) stops in organ playing; as, *jeux forts*, loud stops; *grand jeu*, full organ.

JEW'S HARP, a small instrument made of brass or steel, and shaped as a lyre; when played, it is placed between the teeth, and struck with the fore finger.

JIG, a quick movement in compound time of $\frac{6}{8}$ or $\frac{12}{8}$.

JINGLES, loose pieces of tin placed around a tamborine to increase the sound.

JOCULATOR, (*F.*) strolling musicians.

JONGLEURS, (*F. Pl.*) Itinerant musicians were formerly so called.

JUBE, or JULE, a hymn sung by the Greeks and Romans at harvest time, in honor of Ceres and Bacchus.

JUBILEE. This word is derived from Jubal, the supposed inventor of musical instruments. It was applied by the Hebrews to the year of deliverance, which was proclaimed with the sound of a horn.

JUST, JUSTE, (*F.*) an epithet applied to all consonant intervals, and to those voices, strings, and pipes, which give them with exactness.

JUSTESSE, (*F.*) exactness or purity of intonation.

K.

KABARO, an Egyptian and Abyssinian drum.

KALAMAIKA, a lively Hungarian dance in $\frac{2}{4}$ time.

KAMMER, (*G.*) chamber; as,

————CONCERT, a chamber concert.

————MUSIK, chamber music.

KAPELLMEISTER, (*G.*) a chapel master.

KECKHEIT, (*G.*) boldness; as, *mit keckheit vorge tragen*, with a bold and vigorous style of performance.

KEENERS, the name of the Irish singing mourners.

KEMAN, a Turkish violin with three strings.

KERANIM, Hebrew sacerdotal trumpets.

KERAS, the hydraulica.

KEY, the lever by which the notes of a piano-forte or organ are made to sound. Flutes, hautboys, and other wind instruments have also their keys, by which certain holes are opened or shut. A key is also an assemblage of notes, each of which has a fixed and distinct relation to one particular note, which, for this reason, is called the key-note.

KEY-BOARD, the row of keys of a piano-forte or organ, when spoken of collectively.

——NOTE, a note to which a series of other subordinate notes bears a distinct relation.

KING, an instrument made of stones.

KINOR, (*H.*) the harp of David.

KIRCHEN-MUSIK, (*G.*) church music.

KIT, a small or pocket violin used by dancing masters.

KLANG, (*G.*) sound.

KLANGESCHLECHT, (*G.*) a genus; as, *chromatisches klangeschlecht*, the chromatic genus.

KLAPPE, (*G.*) a key belonging to any wind instrument.

KLAPPEN FLUGELHORN, (*G.*) the keyed bugle.

KLAPPTROMPETE, (*G.*) a keyed trumpet.

KLEIN, (*G.*) minor, in regard to intervals.

KNELL, the sound of the funeral bell.

KREUZ, (*G.*) the character called a *sharp*.

KROUSTA, (*Gk.*) a general name applied by the ancients to all pulsatile instruments.

KRUMHORN, a portable wind instrument formerly much in use, the formation and tone of which resembled a small cornet.

KURZ, (*G.*) short.

KYRIE, (*L.*) Lord. In the Catholic service, the first movement of the mass begins with music set to the words *Kyrie eleison, Christe eleison*, Lord have mercy upon us, Christ have mercy upon us.

L.

L., L. H., indicate the left hand in piano-forte music.

LA, a syllable used in solfaing to the note A.

LA, (*I.* and *F.*) the; as, *la voce*, the voice.

LA CHASSE, (*F.*) a piece of music in the hunting style.

—— VOLTA, a lively dance or tune.

LACRIMOSO, LAGRIMOSO, (*I.*) in a mournful, dolorous style.

L'AME, (*F.*), the sound-post of a violin, tenor, &c.

LAMENTS, name given by the Scotch to some of their old serious and melancholy airs.

LAMENTATIONE, (*I.*) to be sung in a melancholy style.

LAMENTATIONS, the funeral music of the ancient Jews.

LAMENTATRICES, Hebrew female vocal performers, hired to chant over the dead, and to sing dirges at funerals.

LAMENTABILE, LAMENTABILMENTE, LAMENTOSO, LAMENTANDO, LAMENTEVOLMENTE, LAMENTIVOLE, (*I.*) plaintively, mournfully.

LAMPADARIUS, (*Gk.*) the two principal singers in the patriarchal church of Constantinople.

LÄNDLER, (*G.*) a country dance or air in a rustic and popular style, generally in $\frac{3}{8}$ time.

LANDU. See *Lundu.*

LANGSAM, (*G.*) slowly.

LANGUEMENTE, LANGUENDO, (*I.*) languishingly.

LANGUENTE, LANGUIDO, (*I.*) with languor.

LA PRIMA INTENTIONE, (*I.*) the original design of a composer, distinguished by this appellation from an altered or improved copy.

LARGAMENTE, LARGHEZZA, (*I.*) in a full, free, broad style of performance.

LARGE, the name of a note shaped thus,  found in ancient music. It is equal to eight semibreves.

LARGEMENT, (*F.*) very slow.

LARGHETTO, (*I.*) indicates a time slow and measured in its movement, but less so than *largo*.

LARGHISSIMO, (*I.*) extremely slow.

LARGO, (*I.*) a very slow and solemn degree of movement.

———— DI MOLTO, (*I.*) of unusual size.

LARIGOT, (*F.*) an organ stop, tuned an octave above the twelfth.

LARYNX, (*Gk.*) The larynx is composed of five annular cartilages, placed one above another, and united by elastic ligaments, or fibres, by which it is so dilated and contracted as to be capable of producing all the various tones of the voice.

LAUDI, or LODI, name formerly given to certain sacred songs in praise of the Deity.

LAUDAMUS, (*L.*) We praise thee. A part of the mass.

LAUDISTI, or LAUDESI, (*L.*) members of a society instituted at Florence, in 1310, for the performance of the Laudi.

LAUS PERENNIS, (*L.*) a perpetual singing preserved at Antioch by order of the monks. It departed with the vestal fires of antiquity.

LAUF, (*G.*) that part of a violin, tenor, &c., into which the pegs are inserted; also, a rapid succession of notes.

LAUTE, (*G.*) the lute.

LAY, a light, fanciful song.

LE, (*I. Pl.*) the; as, *le voci*, the voices.

LEADER, one who in a concert takes the principal violin, receives the time and style of the several movements from the conductor, and communicates them to the performers.

LEADING NOTE, the seventh note of the scale of any key, when at the distance of a semitone below the key-note.

LEAPS, a distance consisting of several intermediate intervals.

LEANING NOTE, a fore note.

LEBHAFT, (*G.*) lively.

LE CHANTE ROYAL, (*F.*) verses sung to the Virgin and saints by pilgrims from the holy sepulchre.

LEÇON, (*F.*) a lesson. A composition for any instrument of an instructive character.

LEDGER LINES, extra lines added to those of the stave.

LEGATISSIMO, (*I.*) very smoothly connected.

LEGATO, (*I.*) a word implying a close, gliding manner of performance.

LEGATURA, or LEGARE, a binding together.

LEGEREMENT, (*F.*)
LEGGIARDO, (*I.*)
LEGGIEREMENTE, (*I.*)
LEGGIEREZZA, *con*, (*I.*)
} with lightness, gayety.

LEGGIERISSIMO, (*I.*) with the greatest possible facility and lightness of touch and execution.

LEGGIERO, (*I.*) in a light manner.

LEGNO, *col*, (*I.*) with the bow stick.

LEICHT, (*G.*) easy.

LESSON, a word formerly used to signify those exercises which are now called *sonatas*.

LENTANDO, (*I.*) with increased slowness.

LENTEMENT, (*F.*)
LENTEMENTE, (*I.*) } in slow time.
LENTO, (*I.*)

LENTEUR, *avec*, (*F.*)
LENTEZZA, *con*, (*I.*) } with slowness, in a sedate and lingering pace.

LETTURA, (*I.*) reading, as in the case of music.

LEUTO, a musical instrument of the lute kind.

LEVARE, the down beat.

———— ANTIPHONAM, an expression used in the old church music, signifying to begin or open the leading part of the anthem.

LIAISON, (*F.*) smoothness of connection; also, a bind or tie.

LIBERAMENTE, (*I.*) freely, easily.

LIBRETTO, (*I.*) The book of the words of an Italian opera is so called.

LICENSE, a liberty taken in composition or performance, by which the master violates, for a moment, those received rules and regulations which form the established system of harmony and modulation.

LICHANOS, (*Gk.*) the third chord of the two first tetrachords.

———— HYPATON, (*Gk.*) the third sound of the first or lowest tetrachord.

———— MESON, (*Gk.*) the third sound of the *meson*, or middle tetrachord.

LIGHT, a thin, airy composition. The term is also applied to those keys which make but little resistance to the pressure of the fingers.

LIGNE, (*F.*)
LINEA, (*I.*) } a line of the stave.
LINIE, (*G.*)

LIMMA, or REINNART, an interval used in the ancient Greek music, which is less by a comma than a major semitone.

LINK, (*G.*) left; as, *links hand*, the left hand.

LINTO, a small lute.

LINES, those members of a stave on and between which the notes are placed. They were designed by Guido. At their first introduction the spaces between them were not used.

LINOS, a kind of rustic air used by the ancient Greeks, who had also a dirge of the same name.

LIQUID, an epithet metaphorically applied to a smooth succession of the sweet and mellow sounds of any voice or wind instrument; also, to certain clear and sweet tones.

LIRE, (*F.*) to read, as regards music.

LIRA, lyre.

——— GRANDE, (*I.*) the *viol di gamba*, a viol with six strings, formerly much used in Germany, but at present little practised.

LISCIO, highly finished.

L' ISTESSO MOVIMENTO, L' ISTESSO TEMPO, (*I.*) in the same time as the previous movement.

LITTANIA, the litany of the church.

LITTUUS, a staff used by the Angers, in the form of a crosier. It was an instrument that made a shrill or acute sound.

LIUTO, (*I.*) the lute.

LOBGESANG, (*G.*) a hymn, a song of praise.

LOCO. (*L.*) This word implies that a passage is to be played just as it is written, in regard to pitch; it generally occurs after 8*va alta*, or 8*va bassa*.

——— PEDALE. This term denotes that the notes are to be played in the same pitch in which they appear; also, that the pedal is to be used.

LOCRICO, or LOCRENSE, one of the ancient tones or modes.

LONG, the name of a note formerly in use, equal to four semibreves.

LOURE, (*F.*) an old-fashioned French dance.

LOUVRE, (*F.*) a well-known French air, otherwise called *l'aimable vainqueur*, for which Louis XIV. had a remarkable predilection.

LOW, a word of relative signification, and arbitrarily applied to any part, passage, or note situated, towards the bottom of the compass of that species of voice or instrument by which it is designed to be executed.

LUGUBRE, (*I.*) mournfully, sadly.

LUNDU, a Portuguese dance in $\frac{2}{4}$ or $\frac{2}{2}$ time.

LUNGA PAUSA, (*I.*) an expression signifying that the performer must cease playing for a considerable time.

LUNIG, a species of song much used in the Hebrides and Scotland. It is a short, plaintive air, sung by the women at their diversions and work.

LUOGO, or LOCO, in place. To be sung in the way in which they stand. Where a change has been employed, this term signifies that the change terminates.

LUSINGANDO, LUSINGATO, LUSINGHEVOLE, LUSINGHEVOLMENTE, LUSINGHIERO, LUSINGHIERE, (*I.*) soothingly, persuasively.

LUTE, a stringed instrument, formerly much esteemed.

LYCHANOIDES, (*Gk.*) the middle sound of those which Bacchius and other Greek writers call *Spissi.*

LYDIAN, the name of one of the ancient modes.

LYRA, (*I.*) the lyre.

——— DOPPIA, (*I.*) an ancient instrument, not at present known.

——— MENDICORIUM, (*L.*) an ancient instrument, the body of which resembled that of a violin.

——— GUITARRE, (*F.*) a French instrument having six strings, and formed somewhat like an ancient lyre.

———VIOL, an instrument once much in use. It was formed like a viol, had six strings and seven frets or stops, to which were assigned seven letters of the alphabet, viz.: B, C, D, E, F, G, H, the letter A answering to the open string wherever it occurred.

LYRE, one of the most ancient of stringed instruments, and said to have been invented by Mercury, in the year 2000 B. C.

LYRIC, poetry adapted for and intended to be set to music.

LYRICHORD, an ancient stringed instrument.

LYRODI, vocalists among the ancients, who used the lyre in their performances.

LYTIERSE, name given by the ancient Greeks to the song of the reapers.

M.

MA, (*I.*) but; as, *allegro ma non troppo*, quick, but not too much so.

MACHUL, an instrument used by the Hebrews. The name is supposed to have been given to two different instruments, one of the stringed, and the other of the pulsatile species.

MADRIGALE, (*I.*) MADRIGALS, elaborate compositions for voices in five or six parts, in the ancient style of imitation and fugue.

MADRIGALI CONCERTATI, those madrigals that have an accompaniment.

MADRIALE, (*I.*) name formerly given by the Italians to the intermezzi, or pieces performed between the acts of a play or an opera.

MAESTA, *con*, MAESTOSO, (*I.*) with majesty and grandeur.

MAESTRO DI CAPELLA, (*I.*) }
MAITRE DE CHAPELLE, (*F.*) } chapel master, or director of the choir in a chapel in Catholic countries.

MAESTRO DEL CORO, (*I.*) the master of the choir.

MAGADIS, an ancient treble instrument furnished with double strings.

MAGADIZING, a term in the ancient Greek music, signifying a vocal performance in octaves, when men and women, or men and boys, join in the same air.

MAGGIORE, (*I.*) the major key.

MAGODI, (*Gk.*) humorous strolling musicians.

MAGODIS, an ancient instrument having two sets of strings.

MAGGIOLATA, a song for the month of May.

MAGNIFICAT, (*L.*) part of the vespers.

MAIN, (*F.*) the hand; as, *main droite*, *main gauche*, or *M. D.*, *M. G.*, the right or left hand in piano music.

—— DROITE, (*F.*) the right hand.

—— GAUCHE, (*F.*) the left hand.

MAJOR, greater, in respect to intervals and modes.

—— THIRD, a third whose degrees are large seconds.

—— MODE, one of the two modern modes; that in which the third from the key-note is major.

MAJEUR, (*F.*) major, greater — in opposition to minor, less — in respect to scales, intervals, modes, &c.

MALINCONIA, MALINCONICAMENTE, MALINCONICO, (*I.*) in a melancholy style.

MANCA, left hand.

MANCANDO, (*I.*) indicates a gradual decrease in the quantity of tone.

MANCHE, (*F.*) the neck of a violin.

MANDOLINE, (*F.*) }
MANDOLINO, (*I.*) } an instrument with four strings, and with frets, like a guitar; it is tuned like the violin.

MANICO, (*I.*) the neck of a violin, tenor, &c.

MANICHORD, a stringed instrument, somewhat resembling a spinet.

MANIEREN, (*G. Pl.*) graces, embellishments.

MANO, (*I.*) the hand; as,

——— DRITTA, (*I.*) the right hand.

——— SINISTRA, (*I.*) the left hand.

MANUAL, (*G.*) the key-board.

MANUALE. This term is used to designate the hand keys of an organ, or any instrument having foot keys, in contradistinction to the latter.

MANU DUCTOR, (*L.*) name given by the ancients to the officiate whose province it was to beat time with his hand.

MARCATO, (*I.*) in a marked and emphatic style.

MARCATISSIMO, (*I.*) very strongly marked.

MARCH, a military air or movement composed for drums, trumpets, and other martial instruments.

MARCHE, (*F.*) a march In harmony, a symmetrical sequence of chords.

MARCIA, (*I.*) } a march.
MARSCH, (*G.*) }

MARCIA CON MOTO, a quick march.

MARTELLANDO, (*I.*) strongly marking, or, as it were, hammering the notes.

MARTELLARE, (*I.*) to strike the notes so as to imitate the blow of a hammer.

MARTELLATO, (*I.*) forcibly marked, hammered.

MARZIALE, (*I.*) in a martial style.

MASRAKITHA, a pneumatic instrument used by the ancient Hebrews, composed of pipes of various dimensions, fitted into a wooden chest open at the top, and stopped at the bottom with wood covered with a skin.

MASCHARADA, buffoonery music.

MASK, MASQUE, a sort of musical drama or operetta performed by characters in masks.

MASS, a Catholic musical service, consisting of several movements.

MÄSSIG, (*G.*) moderately; as, *mässig langsam*, moderately slow.

MASURE, MASURECK, MASURKA, MAZOURK, MAZURKA, MAZURECK, (*G.*) a quick Polish dance in $\frac{3}{8}$ time, with a peculiar rhythmic construction, somewhat like that of the polacca.

MATINS, (*F.*) the early morning service in convents and Catholic churches.

MATINATA, a song for the morning.

MATERIA MUSICA, matters relating to music.

MAXIMA, or MASSIMA, the note called a *largo*.

MEAN, a term formerly applied to the tenor or medium part in compositions for several voices, male and female.

——— CLEF, tenor clef.

MEASURE, that division of time by which the air and motion of music are regulated.

MEDESSIMO, (*I.*) the same.

————— TEMPO, (*I.*) in the same time.

MEDIANT, the third note of the scale.

MEDIANTE, (*F.*) the mediant or third note of the scale.

MEDITATIO, (*L.*) the middle of a chant.

MEDLEY, an assemblage of detached parts or passages of different well-known songs, so arranged that the latter words of the line of one part connects with the beginning of that of another song.

MELANGE, (*F.*) a composition founded on several favorite airs; a medley.

MELODY, a series of single sounds, so arranged as to produce a varied and agreeable effect on the ear.

MELODIA. (*I.*) } melody.
MELODIE, (*F.*) }

MELODIOUS, a term applied to any pleasing succession of sounds given in time and measure; also, to clear-toned voices.

MELODIOSA, (*I.*) melodious.

MELODICS, forms of study relating to the general nature of melody.

MELODIZE, so to arrange words that their pronunciation is melodious.

MELODISAMENTE, harmoniously, or in just melody.

MELODIAL MODULATION, a change from one key to another, produced by the result of successive melodic intervals.

MELODRAMA, } a species of pantomimic drama, in which
MELODRAME, (*F.*) } much of the interest depends upon de-
MELODRAMMA, (*I.*) } scriptive instrumental music.

MELOS, (*Gk.*) a term applied by the ancients to the sweetness of any melody, or to that quality or character by which a melody was rendered agreeable.

MELOPOIA, (*Gk.*) a term in ancient music, signifying the art or rules of composition.

MELOPOMENOS, vocal melody.

MEME, (*F.*) the same.

——— MOUVEMENT, (*F.*) in the same time.

MEN., (*I.*) an abbreviation of the word *meno*, less; as, *men forte* less loud, *men vivo*, with less spirit.

——— FORTE, (*I.*) less loud.

MENESTRAUDIE, (*F.*) a company of minstrels.

MENO, (*I.*) less.

MESSA, (*I.*) a mass or Catholic musical service.

——— CONCERTATA, (*I.*) a concerted mass.

——— DI VOCE, (*I.*) a swelling and diminishing of the voice on a long-holding note.

MESAULICI, (*Gk.*) pieces performed between the divisions of the Greek drama.

MESCOLOMENTO, or **MISTIO**, (*Gk.*) rules for so arranging the sounds of a melody that the voice or instrument might be kept within a certain compass.

MESCOLANZA, a combination of secular and ecclesiastical music.

MESE, (*Gk.*) a name given by the Greeks to the central string of the lyre, but more commonly denoting the sound which was the centre of their system of tetrachords.

MESOCHORI, (*Gk.*) musicians among the ancients who presided at public performances, and directed the time by beating with their feet, on which they wore wooden shoes.

MESOLABE, (*Gk.*) an instrument for dividing time into equal parts.

MESOPYCNI, (*Gk.*) the second sound in each tetrachord.

MESONYCTICON, midnight singing of the early Christians.

MESOIDES, (*Gk.*) a kind of melopœia, the sounds of which were chiefly confined to the middle chords.

MESSE, (*F.*) a mass, or Catholic musical service.

MESTO, (*I.*) mournfully, sadly, pathetically.

MESTOSO, (*I.*) sadly, pensively.

MESURE, (*F.*) the bar or measure.

——— A DEUX TEMS, (*F.*) common time.

——— TROIS TEMS, (*F.*) triple time.

METALLICO, (*I.*) of a metallic quality.

METHODE, (*F.*) a treatise or book of instructions

METEDO, (*I.*) method.

METRE, (*F.*) measure.

METRICS, the measure adopted in poetry and music.

METRONOME, (*F.*) an ingenious instrument for indicating the exact time of a musical piece, by means of a pendulum, which may be shortened or lengthened at pleasure.

METRUM, (*G.*) the measure or time.

MEZZA, (*I.*) the feminine of *mezzo*, indicating a medium, in the middle, or half.

——— **BRAVURA**, (*I.*) a song of moderate difficulty as to execution.

——— **MANICA**, (*I.*) the half-shift, in violin playing.

——— **VOCE**, (*I.*) with a moderate tone and manner.

MEZZO, (*I.*) half; as, *mezzo voce*, in a subdued tone; *mezzo piano*, rather soft; *mezzo forte*, rather loud.

——— **CARATTERE**, (*I.*) an expression applied to songs of a middle character, songs neither insipidly plain nor highly ornamental.

——— **FORTE**, (*I.*) rather loud.

——— **PIANO**, (*I.*) rather soft.

——— **SOPRANO**, (*I.*) a female voice of a lower pitch than the soprano or treble. A C clef for this voice used to be placed on the second line of the stave.

——— **TRILLO**, (*I.*) a sixteenth note.

——— **TENORE**, (*I.*) half tenor.

——— **TUONO**, (*I.*) a semitone.

MI, (*I.*) a syllable used in solfaing to designate E, or the third note of the major scale.

— **CONTRA FA**, (*L.*) terms applied by ancient theorists to all false relations between the notes of one chord as compared with the notes of that which immediately preceded or followed it.

MIGNON, (*F.*) favorite.

MILITARMENTE, (*I.*) in a military style.

MIMES, singing mimics, once in great repute.

MINAGNGHINIM, a pulsatile instrument used by the Hebrews, consisting of a square table of wood furnished with a handle; over this table was stretched an iron chain, or hempen cord, passing through balls of wood or brass, which, striking against the table, produced a clear sound heard at a great distance.

MINACCIOSO, MINACCIANDO, (*I.*) in a threatening style.

MINEUR, (*F.*) minor, in speaking of keys and intervals.

MINIM, a note of which the duration is equal to one half of the semibreve.

——— REST, half note rest.

MINIMA, minim.

MINOR, less, in regard to intervals.

——— MODE, that of the only two modes recognized in modern music in which the third degree of the scale from the tonic forms the interval of a minor third.

——— CANONS, certain clergymen of the church of England, who occasionally assist in the performance of the service and anthem.

MINORE, (*I.*) less, in respect to intervals; minor, as to modes and keys.

MINSTRELS, itinerant bards or poet-musicians, who flourished in the tenth and eleventh centuries.

MINSTRELSY, the performance of a minstrel.

MINUET, a movement in $\frac{4}{3}$ measure, of a slow and graceful motion, and always beginning with the beating note; this is a dancing minuet. There are others of a time somewhat quicker, and which were formerly much used as concluding movements of overtures, sonatas, &c. When thus employed, it is usually marked *scherzo*.

MINUE, or MINUETTO. See *Minuet*.

MISERERE, (*L.*) Have mercy. A psalm of supplication.

MISSA, (*L.*) a mass. In a musical sense, the mass consists of five principal movements — the Kyrie, Gloria, Credo, Sanctus, and Agnus Dei.

MISSAL, an abridgment of the chants introduced into the Catholic service by Gregory the Great.

MISTERIOSAMENTE, MISTERIOSO, (*I.*) in a mysterious manner.

MISURATO, (*I.*) in measured or strict time.

MIT, (*G.*) with; as, *mit begleitung*, with an accompaniment.

MITTELSTIMMEN, (*G. Pl.*) the middle parts.

MIXED CADENCE, the triad on the subdominant followed by that on the dominant.

MIXOLYDIAN, the name of one of the ancient modes.

MIXTURE, an organ stop, consisting of two or more ranks of pipes.

MOBILE, name given by the Greeks to the two middle chords of each tetrachord.

MOCIGANGA, (*S.*) a musical interlude common in Spain.

MODE, a certain arrangement of tones and semitones.

MODERATAMENTE, MODERATO, MODERAZIONE, *con*, (*I.*) with a moderate degree of quickness.

MODERATISSIMO, (*I.*) in very moderate time.

MODESTO, (*I.*) modestly, quietly.

MODINHA, a short Portuguese song.

MODO, (*I.*) a mode; as,

—— MAGGIORE, (*I.*) the major mode.

—— MINORE, (*I.*) the minor mode.

MODULATION, a change of key.

MODULAZIONE, (*I.*) modulation.

MODUS, (*L.*) mode.

MOLL, (*G.*) minor, in relation to modes and keys; as, *A moll*, A minor; *H moll*, B minor.

MOLLEMENTE, (*I.*) softly, effeminately.

MOLTO, (*I.*) very, extremely; as, *molto allegro*, very quick; *molto adagio*, extremely slow.

—— ADAGIO, (*I.*) extremely slow.

—— ALLEGRO, (*I.*) very quick.

—— MOSSO, (*I.*) with quick emotion.

—— SOSTENUTO, (*I.*) in a manner very much sustained.

—— VIBRATO, very violent or rapid.

—— VOCE, with full voice.

MOLLE, (*F.*) This word, used as a musical term, signifies that the tone is a small second or half degree lower than its usual pitch.

MOLOSSUS, three long or the same number of accented notes immediately following each other, composing a musical foot.

MONAULOS, (*Gk.*) a kind of single flute, of higher antiquity than even the lyre. Its shape was crooked, and something like that of a bull's horn.

MONFERINA, (*I.*) a very lively dance in $\frac{6}{8}$ time.

MONOCHORD, an instrument with one string, for elucidating the doctrine of intervals.

MONOCORDO, (*I.*)
MONOCORDE, A, (*F.*) } on only one string.

8*

MONODIA, MONODIE, (*I.*) MONODY, a term anciently applied to a melody intended to be performed by a single voice.

MONODIC, resembling or possessing the nature of a monody.

MONODICA, (*I.*) See *Monody.*

MONOPHONIC. See *Monodia.*

MONOLOGUE, a poem, song, or scene, written and composed for a single performer.

MONOTONOUS, an epithet applied to any instrument which produces but one tone or note.

MONTANT, (*F.*) ascending.

MORALIZATIONS, name given to certain old Scotch puritanical songs.

MORCEAU, (*F.*) a piece or musical composition of any kind.

MORDENTE, (*I.*) a grace formed by two or more notes preceding the principal note.

MORRICE-DANCE, a dance once much practised by soldiery; its movements are accompanied with the sound of bells and clashing swords.

MORISCO, *alla*, (*I.*) in the Moorish style.

MORENDO, (*I.*) gradually diminishing the sound till it dies away, and at the same time slackening the time.

MORMORANDO, (*I.*) murmuring.

MOSSO, (*I.*) movement; as, *piu mosso,* quicker movement; *meno mosso,* slower movement.

MOSTRA, (*I.*) a direct.

MOTETTO, (*I.*) a piece of sacred music for several voices.

MOTIVO, (*I.*) a subject for a fugue or other composition.

MOTO, *con,* (*I.*) with agitation. This word is sometimes added to the Italian word denoting the speed of the movement; as, *andante con moto.*

MOTO CONTRARIO, (*I.*) in contrary movement. A term used in counterpoint to imply that the melody of one part moves in an opposite direction to that of another.

MOTTEGGIANDO, (*I.*) jeeringly, jocosely.

MOTUS, (*L.*) motion; as,

——— CONTRARIUS, (*L.*) contrary motion.

——— OBLIQUUS, (*L.*) oblique motion.

——— RECTUS, (*L.*) similar or direct motion.

MOUTHPIECE, the part of a trumpet or similar instrument which is placed in the mouth while performing.

MOVEMENT, a strain of music, or a connected passage.

MOVIMENTO, (*I.*) time, movement.

MUSE, name originally given to the muzzle or tube of the bagpipe.

MUSETTE, the name of a small bagpipe, the performers on which were called *musars*; also, an air generally written in common time, of a soft and soothing character; also, a dance of similar style.

MUSARS, performers on the musette.

MUSIC, the language of sounds.

MUSICAL GLASSES, several glasses tuned to the notes of the scale, and composing the harmonica, an instrument invented by Dr. Franklin.

MUSICA ANTIQUA, the music of the Greeks and Romans down to the eleventh century.

——— ARITHMETICA, that part of musical science which considers sounds by the help of numbers.

——— ARTIFICIALE, music that is not performed by the natural organs of the voice, but by instruments.

——— ALLIVA, that part of musical science which regards only the execution, without considering the reasons or cause of the good effect of such execution.

——— CHORAICA, dancing music.

——— CHORALE, the music of a chorus or chant.

——— CHROMATICA, a style of music in which there are many chromatic signs.

——— COMBINATORIA, that which teaches the manner of combining the sounds, or rightly joining them in as many different manners as possible.

——— CONTEMPLATIVA, SPECULATIVA, or THEORICA, the treatment of sounds, examination of their natures, properties, and effects, without regard to the executive part.

——— DIATONICA, a species of music, the scale whereof proceeds by tones and semitones. It is one of the genera of the ancients, and is thought to be the first, on account of its being so easy and natural.

——— DIDACTICA, a speculative consideration of the quantity, proportions, and different qualities of sound.

——— DRAMATICA, SCENICA, or THEATRALE, music arranged for theatrical effect.

MUSICA ECCLESIASTICA, or DI CHIESA, for the church.

——— ENHARMONICA, that wherein the enharmonic diesis was frequently used.

——— FIGURALIS, FIGURATA, or COLORATA, figurative music, wherein the notes are of different value, and the motions of various time.

——— HARMONICA, a piece consisting of many parts, which, though very different, when played together, make a very agreeable whole.

——— HISTORICA, a treatment of the origin and invention of music, its modes, notes, instruments, &c.; also, the lives and writings of authors on the subject.

——— INSTRUMENTALIS, instrumental music.

——— MANIEROSA, music adapted in its style to the manners of the people.

——— MELISMATICA, or MELODICA, the most correct arrangement of music, according to the rules of melody.

——— MELOPOETICA, the art of ranging and disposing sound in an agreeable manner.

——— METRICA, the harmonious cadence of the voice.

——— NATURALE, vocal music.

——— PATHETICA, a moving and affecting kind of music, that touches and causes emotions in the mind, of love, sorrow, pity, or any other passion.

MUSIC OF THE SPHERES, that harmony supposed by the ancients to result from the orderly motion of the heavenly bodies.

MUSICO, (*I.*) a musician; also, the name applied to those male vocalists who formerly sang the soprano parts in operas, &c.

MUTE, a small instrument which is occasionally placed on the bridge of a violin, tenor, or violoncello, to damp or diminish the tone of the instrument by checking its vibrations.

MUTATION, change; as a musical term it refers to the transition of voice at an early age.

MYLOTHROS, (*Gk.*) the millers' and bakers' song.

N.

NACCARE, (*I.*) the castanets.

NACAIRE, (*F.*) a kind of brazen drum, formerly much used in France and Italy.

NACHAHMUNG, (*G.*) imitation.

NACHDRUCK, (*G.*) emphasis, accent.

NACHSPIEL, (*G.*) a postlude, or piece played after some other.

NACHSTVERWANDTE TÖNE, (*G.*) nearest relative keys.

NAKOKUS, name of an instrument much used by the Egyptians in their Coptic churches and religious processions, consisting of two brass plates suspended by strings, and struck together, by way of beating time.

NAKED. This word is applied to a number of notes when those that complete the chord are wanting.

NASAL TONE. In singing, this term implies that the voice is deteriorated by passing through the nostrils.

NASARD, an organ stop, tuned a twelfth above the diapasons.

NATURAL, the character which restores a note, that has been sharpened or flattened, to its original state.

——— **HARMONY,** that produced by the natural and essential chords of the mode.

——— **MODULATION,** that which is confined to the key of the piece and its relatives.

NATIONAL SONGS, songs that are identified with the history of a nation, or the manners and customs of its people.

NAUTICAL SONGS, songs relating to the customs of seafaring life.

NEAPOLITAN SIXTH, a chord composed of a minor third and minor sixth, which is situated on the fourth degree of the scale. In the key of C major or minor this chord is as follows: D♭, A♭, F.

NEANES, one of the eight barbarous terms used by the modern Greeks in their ecclesiastical music.

NEBEL, or **NEBEL NASSOR,** (*H.*) the name given by the ancient Jews to their harp, mentioned in the Psalms as "an instrument of ten strings."

NEBENGEDANKEN (*G. Pl.*) accessory and subordinate ideas.

NECK, that part of a violin, guitar, &c., extending from the head to the body, and on which the finger-board is fixed.

NECESSARIO signifies that the passage near which it is placed must not be omitted.

NEGHINOTH, (*H.*) stringed instruments.

NEGLIGENTE, NEGLIGENTEMENTE, NEGLIGENZA, *con,*

(*I.*) negligently; without restraint or strict attention to the order of the piece.

NEGLI, NEI, NEL, NELLA, NELLE, NELLO, (*I.*) in the.

NETTAMENTE, NETTO, (*I.*) neatly.

NETE, (*Gk.*) name given by the Greeks to the fourth, or most acute chord of each of the three tetrachords which followed the two first or deepest.

—— DIEZEUGMENON, (*Gk.*) the final or highest sound of the fourth tetrachord.

—— HYPERBOLAEON, (*Gk.*) the last sound of the highest tetrachord.

—— SYNEMMENON, (*Gk.*) the fourth sound of the third tetrachord when conjoint with the second.

NETOIDES, highest note of the ancient scale.

NEUMAE, (*L.*) a term applied by old musicians to divisions upon a single vowel at the end of a psalm or anthem, as a recapitulation of the whole melody.

NEUVIEME, (*F.*) the interval of a ninth.

NIEDERSCHLAG, (*G.*) the accented part of a bar.

NINTH, an interval containing an octave and a second.

NINETEENTH, an interval containing two octaves and a fifth.

NOBILE, NOBILIMENTE, (*I.*) with nobleness; grandeur.

NOCTURNO, (*I.*) } NOCTURNE, (*F.*) } same as *Notturno*. A vocal or instrumental composition, of a light, fanciful character, suitable for an evening recreation.

NOELS, name given by the French to their Christmas carols.

NOENTA, name given by the ancients to their dirge or funeral song.

NOIRE, (*F.*) a crotchet.

NOMES, (*Gk.*) certain airs in the ancient music sung to Cybele, the mother of the gods. It was also applied to every air, the composition of which was regulated by certain determined and inviolable rules.

NOMION, (*Gk.*) the appellation given by the Greeks to a kind of love song.

NOMODICTAI, (*L.*) the name given by the ancient Romans to the umpires at their sacred games and musical contests.

NON, (*I.*) an adverb of negation, generally associated with *troppo*; as,

NON TROPPO ALLEGRO, NON TROPPO PRESTO, (*I.*) not too quick.

—— MOLTO, (*I.*) not very much; as, *non molto allegro*, not very quick.

—— TANTO, (*I.*) not too much; as, *allegro non tanto*, not too quick.

NONA, (*I.*) the interval of a ninth.

NONETTO, (*I.*) a composition in nine parts.

NONUPLA, a quick species of time, consisting of nine crotchets or nine quavers in a bar.

NOTA, (*L.*) a note. Of these we have various kinds; as,

—— BUONA, an accented note.

—— CATTIVA, an unaccented note.

—— CAMBIATA, a note of irregular transition.

—— CARRATTERISTICA, a leading or characteristic note.

—— DI PASSAGIO, (*I.*)
NOTE DE PASSAGE, (*F.*) } a passing note, or note of regular transition.

NOTA D' ABELLIMENTO, (*I.*)
NOTE D'AGREMENT, (*F.*) } a note of irregular transition.

NOTA INTIERA, (*I.*) whole note.

—— SENSIBILE, (*I.*)
—— SENSIBILIS, (*L.*)
NOTE SENSIBLE, (*F.*) } the leading note of the scale, or that note of the scale which is situated a semitone below the key-note.

NOTATION, the art of representing musical sounds and their various modifications by notes, signs, terms, &c.

NOTAZIONE MUSICALE, (*I.*) musical notation.

NOTES, (*L.*) characters, which by their various forms and situations on the staves, indicate the duration, as well as the gravity or acuteness, of the several sounds of a composition.

NOTE ANTICIPATE, note of anticipation, or that which is sounded prior to others of the chord to which it belongs.

—— OF MODULATION, that which introduces a new key.

—— —— PROLATION, (*L.*) a dotted note.

—— RITARDTE, a retarding note; the reverse of *note anticipate*.

NOTENPLAN, (*G.*) the stave.

NOTES DE GOUT, (*F.*) notes of embellishment.

NOTHUS, an epithet applied by the ancient Greeks to the Hyper-Æolian and Hyper-Phrygian modes.

NOTTURNO, (*I.*) a composition, vocal or instrumental, suitable for evening recreation, from its elegance and lightness of character.

NOUVELLE METHODE, (*F.*) a new method.

NUNNIA, (*Gk.*) name given by the Greeks to the lullaby songs of the nurses.

NUOVO, *di*, (*I.*) newly, again.

O.

O, (*I.*) or; as, *flauto o violino*, flute or violin.

OBBLIGATI, (*Pl.*) OBBLIGATO, (*I.*) a part or parts of a composition indispensable to its just performance, and which, therefore, cannot properly be omitted.

OBLIQUE, a term applied to that relative motion between two parts, where the one ascends or descends, while the other remains stationary.

OBOE, (*I.*) the hautboy. OBOI, hautboys.

OBOISTA, (*I.*) an oboist, a performer of the oboe.

OCTAVE, an interval of eight notes.

——— FLUTE, a flute whose tones range an octave higher than those of the German.

——— STOP, an organ or piano stop having within its compass tones an octave above corresponding ones.

OCTAVINA, the name of an old stringed instrument, comprehending about three octaves.

OCTACHORD, an instrument comprising eight sounds, or seven degrees.

OCTUOR, (*F.*) a piece in eight parts.

ODE, (*Gk.*) an air or song. It is of ancient invention, and consists of unequal verses, distinguished into stanzas or strophes. The ancient ode had originally but one stanza or strophe, but at last was divided into three parts, *strophe*, *antistrophe*, and *epode*. The priests, going round the altar to sing the praises of the gods, called the first entrance *strophe*, the turning towards the altar *antistrophe*, and lastly, standing before the altar, they sung the remainder, which they called the *epode*.

ODEUM, (*Gk.*) } a place for the public performance of music; a
ODEON, } concert room or hall.

ODICUM, (*Gk.*) that part of practical music among the Greeks which concerned vocal performance.

ŒUVRE, (*F.*) opera or work. *Œuvre premier*, the first work, &c.

OFFERTOIRE, (*F.*)
OFFERTORIUM, (*L.*) } a part of the Catholic morning service.
OFFERTORY,

OFICLEIDA, (*I.*) the *serpente*, a French bass-horn.

OFFERTORIO, old name for a motet, or sacred composition for three, five, or more voices.

OHNE, (*G.*) without; as, *ohne begleitungen*, without accompaniments.

OMNES, (*L.*) all, or all together.

ONDEGGIAMENTO, (*I.*) with a waving, tremulous motion of the sound; as also, on the violin, tenor, &c., a close shake.

ONDEGGIARE, or **ONDEGGIARE LA MANO**, (*I.*) an expression signifying that the hand in beating time, or the voice in singing, must wave.

ONGLEUR, name formerly given to performers on the lyre, cithara, harp, lute, and guitar.

ONGARESE, (*I.*) a musical term, which refers to a dance after the Hungarian mode.

OPEN. The strings of an instrument when not pressed are said to be open. The word is also applied to the tones produced on such strings.

——— **DIAPASON**, an organ stop, the pipes of which are open at the top, and generally made of metal. This is the most important stop in the instrument.

——— **HARMONY**, harmony of which the notes are separated by wide intervals.

——— **STOP**, that which regulates the open pipes.

——— **PLAIN SHAKE**, a moderately quick shake of readily distinguished changes, and closing without a turn.

——— **TURNED SHAKE**, similar to *open plain shake*, with the difference that it ends with a turn.

OPERA, (*I.*) a musical drama, consisting of recitatives, airs, choruses, &c., combined with scenery, decorations, and action. This term is also applied to any publication or work of an author.

——— **BUFFA**, (*I.*) a comic opera.

OPERA SEMI-SERIA, (*I.*) a semi-serious opera.

——— SERIA, (*I.*) a serious or tragic opera.

OPERETTA, (*I.*) a short or little opera.

OPERATICAL, relating to the opera.

OPHICLEIDE, a brass instrument lately introduced into this country, of a loud tone and a deep pitch. It is chiefly used in military music.

OPPOSITIONE, or OPPOSIZZIONE, placing one thing against another, or in a place in which it does not belong.

ORATORIO, (*I.*) a musical drama, founded on some scriptural story, performed without the aid of scenery and action.

ORATORICAL, in the style of an oratorio.

ORCHESTRA, (*I.*) that enclosed part of the theatre between the stage and the audience, which is occupied by the musicians or instrumental performers. Sometimes, also, it is applied to designate, collectively, the performers themselves; as, a full orchestra, a thin orchestra.

ORCHESTRAL, relating to the orchestra.

ORDINE, (*I.*) the arrangement of many parts to make a whole one.

ORDINARIO, (*I.*) usual; as, *a tempo ordinario*, in the usual time.

ORECCHIA, ORECCHIO, (*I.*) the ear.

——— MUSICALE, (*I.*)
OREILLE MUSICALE, (*F.*) } a musical ear.

ORGAN,
ORGANO, (*I.*)
ORGEL, (*G.*)
ORGUE, (*F.*) } a well-known and highly-appreciated musical instrument, chiefly used in churches and other places of worship or assemblage.

ORGANIST, a performer on the organ.

ORGANISTIC, relating to the organ. It was also applied to Romish priests who *organized* or sung in parts.

ORGANISTS OF THE HALLELUJAH, an appellation given about the year 1200 to certain priests, or clerks, who assisted in the performance of the mass.

ORGANARII, ancients who performed on the hydraulic organ.

ORGAN BELLOWS, a well-known pneumatic machine attached to an organ, the office of which is to supply the pipes with wind.

——— MUSIC, music expressly composed for the organ, or in the performance of which the use of that instrument is required.

ORGANIZARE, to sing in parts.

ORGANO, (*I.*) a word found in the scores of oratorio choruses, instrumental anthems, &c., at the beginning of that stave designed for the organ, and the execution of the thorough-bass.

——— **PICCIOLO**, (*I.*) a small organ.

ORGANORUM INTABULATURÆ, the general name formerly given to voluntaries, preludes, and all compositions for the organ.

ORGAN STOP, any single set of organ pipes.

——— **PIPES**, the square and cylindrical tubes in an organ, from which proceed the various sounds of the instrument.

——— **POINT**, a long or stationary bass note, upon which various passages of melody and harmony are introduced.

ORGANUM, (*L.*) an ancient species of counterpoint, in fourths, fifths, and octaves.

ORGELGEHÄUSE, (*G.*) the case of an organ.

ORGEL SCHULE, (*G.*) a school or method for the organ.

——— **STÜCKE**, (*G.*) pieces for the organ.

ORGELPUNKT, (*G.*) an organ point or pedal notes.

ORISCUS, the name of one of the ten notes used in the middle ages.

ORNAMENTI, (*I.*) } graces, embellishments, &c.
ORNEMENS, (*F.*) }

ORPHARION, an ancient stringed instrument.

ORTHIAN, (*Gk.*) a term applied by the ancients to a dactylic nome or song, said to have been invented by Phrygian Olympus.

——— **MODE**, in the Orthian style; quick, and particularly pleasing on account of its life and spirit.

ORNEMENS, (*F.*) graces; as, the appoggiatura, turn, shake, &c.

O SIA, (*I.*) or else; as, *o sia più facile*, or else in this more easy manner.

OSSERVANZA, or **CON OSSERVANZA**, (*I.*) with scrupulous exactness in regard to time.

OSTINATO, (*I.*) persevered in, adhered to, continued in despite of circumstances.

OTACOUSTICS, (*Gk.*) instruments that add to or increase the sense of hearing.

OTETTO, (*I.*) a composition in eight parts.

OTTAVA, or 8va, (*I.*) an octave. This word is generally joined with *alta* or *bassa;* the first signifies that the passage to which it is applied must be played an octave higher than it is written; the second, that it must be played an octave lower.

OTTAVINA, (*I.*) the little or higher octave.

OUÏE, (*F.*) the hearing.

OUVERTURE, (*F.*) } an overture, or introductory symphony to a
OVERTURA, (*I.*) } dramatic performance.

OVERTURE, the introductory symphony to an oratorio, opera, &c., and generally consisting of three or four different movements.

OXIPYCNI, (*Gk.*) the name given by the ancients to high sounds in general.

OXYPHONOS, (*Gk.*) the person who sings the highest part.

P.

PÆAN, a song of victory sung by the ancient Greeks in honor of the gods, but chiefly of Mars and Apollo.

PAGINA, a page or folio.

PALCO, (*I.*) a theatrical stage.

PALMULA, (*L.*) the keys of an instrument.

PANARMONION, (*Gk.*) a wind instrument used by the ancient Greeks, consisting of an assemblage of pipes, resembling, in some degree, the organ. It is particularly worthy of notice that every hole of these pipes was capable of emitting three different sounds, and in some circumstances more than three.

PANDEAN PIPES, PAN'S PIPES, one of the most ancient and simple of musical instruments, made of reeds of different lengths, stopped at the bottom, and blown by the mouth at the top.

PANDORA, a stringed instrument, used by the ancients.

PANDORAN, an ancient stringed instrument resembling a lute, the strings of which are of brass.

PANTOMIME, (*Gk.*) a species of musical entertainment, so called because it is all mimic.

PANTING BELLOWS, an improved kind of organ bellows, which give a regular flow of wind to the pipes.

PANTALON, (*F.*) one of the movements of the quadrille. Also, the name of an instrument of the dulcimer species, but larger, and played in the same manner.

PARA, (*Gk.*) a conjunctive word, signifying near; as *para-mese*, near the middle chord.

PARADIAZEUXIS, (*Gk.*) an interval between two tetrachords, consisting of one tone.

PARAMESE, (*Gk.*) the second sound of the second octave.

PARANETE DIAZEUGMENON, (*Gk.*) the third sound of the fourth tetrachord.

——— **HYPERBOLÆON,** (*Gk.*) the penultima of the supreme, or fifth tetrachord.

——— **SYNEMMENON,** (*Gk.*) the last sound but one of the third tetrachord.

PARAPHONIA, (*Gk.*) a word which, with the ancients, was in some degree synonymous with harmony.

PARAPHONOI, (*Gk.*) certain combinations in the ancient music, which were neither concords nor discords, but between both. The moderns have no sounds of the kind.

PARATRIPEMATA, (*Gk.*) name given by the ancients to the side apertures of their flutes.

PARADOXUS, (*Gk.*) the winner of a prize in the musical games of the ancients.

PARACONTACION, alternating singing, formerly much in vogue in the Greek church.

PARODY, or **PARODIA,** in music, signifying that new words are put to an old musical composition.

PARALLEL MOTION. When two parts continue on the same degree, and only repeat the same sounds, they are said to be in parallel motion.

PARFAIT, (*F.*) perfect, with regard to intervals, &c.

PARHYPATE MESON, (*Gk.*) the second sound of the second tetrachord.

PARLANDO, (*I.*) in a speaking or declamatory manner.

PARLANTE, (*I.*) accented, as if with words, in a declamatory style.

PARTE, (*I.*) a part in vocal or instrumental music.

——— **CANTANTE,** (*I.*) the singing or vocal part.

PARTIE, (*F.*) a part in a composition.

PARTIAL TURN, a turn consisting of the chief note and three fore notes, the leading one of which may be either a large or small second above the principal.

PARTIMENTI, (*I. Pl.*) preparatory exercises for the study of harmony and accompaniment.

PARTITION, (*F.*)
PARTITUR, (*G.*)
PARTITURA, (*I.*)
PARTIZIONE, (*I.*) } a score or entire draught of a composition in several parts.

PARTHENIA, (*Gk.*) songs sung by a chorus of virgins at a festival.

PARYPATE HYPATON, (*Gk.*) second note of the lowest tetrachord of the ancients.

PAS, (*F.*) a dance; as, *pas seul, pas de deux,* a dance by one, or by two performers; *pas redoublé,* a quick step.

PASSACAGLIO, (*I.*)
PASSACAILLE, (*F.*) } a slow dance in $\frac{3}{4}$ time.

PASSAGE, any phrase, or short portion of an air, or other composition. Every member of a strain or movement is a passage.

PASSAGGIO, (*I.*) a passage or series of quick notes.

PASSAMEZZO, a slow, simple dance tune.

PASSEPIED, an old French dance in $\frac{3}{8}$ or $\frac{3}{4}$ time.

PASSING-NOTES, notes foreign to the harmony, but which serve to connect those which are essential.

——— SHAKE, a short trill, made in flowing passages of quavers or semiquavers, without breaking the time, or interrupting the natural course of the melody.

——— CHORDS, chords introduced for the purpose of forming an easy transition from one chord to another.

PASSION MUSIC, the music composed in Italy and other Roman Catholic countries expressly for Passion week.

PASSIONATAMENTE, PASSIONATE, (*I.*) in an impassioned manner.

PASSIONATO, PASSIONE, *con,* (*I.*) impassioned, with pathos.

PASSIONE, (*I.*) the passion, or seven last words of our Savior set to music.

PASTICCIO, (*I.*) an opera made up of songs by different masters

PASTORALE, (*I.*) a soft rural movement.

PASTOURELLE, (*F.*) one of the movements of the quadrille

PASTICHE. See *Pasticcio.*

PAUKEN, (*G. Pl.*) the kettle-drums.

PAUSA, (*I.*) a rest.

——— GENERALE, (*I.*) a pause for all the performers

PAUSE, (*F.*) a semibreve, or whole bar's rest.
——— (*G.*) a rest.
——— a musical character, consisting of a dot surmounted by a curve, which serves to protract the duration of a note or rest beyond its natural length.
——— GÉNÉRALE, (*F.*) a term signifying that all the performers are to pause.
PAVANE, (*F.*) an antiquated French dance of a serious cast.
PEALS, as a musical term, a melody composed for bells.
PECTIS, an ancient stringed instrument.
PEDALE, (*I.*) a pedal or stationary bass. In piano music, this term implies that the performer must press down the pedal which takes off the dampers.
——— (*G.*) that set of keys belonging to an organ which are played on by the feet.
——— NOTE, a holding note, during which the harmony formed by the other parts of the composition is allowed to proceed.
——— BASSE, pedal basses.
PEDALI, (*I.*) the pedals in piano or organ music.
PEDALIERA, (*I.*) the pedal keys of an organ, spoken of collectively.
PENTACHORD, a scale of five diatonic degrees.
PENTATONON, (*Gk.*) an interval of five whole tones, or the augmented sixth.
PER, (*I.*) for, or by; as, *per il violino*, for the violin.
—— BISCANTUM, (*L.*) an expression by which the old ecclesiastical musicians signified the composition and performance of music to be in two parts.
PERCUSSIONE, (*I.*) percussion, or the act of striking a note or chord.
PERDENDO, PERDENDOSI, PERDEN., *abb.*, (*I.*) These terms imply a gradual diminution, both in the quantity of tone and speed of movement.
PERFECT, a term applied by theorists to certain intervals and chords.
——— CADENCE, a complete and satisfactory close in both the harmony and melody.
——— CONCORDS, PERFECT CONSONANCES, the perfect fourth, fifth, and eighth.

PERFECT CHORD, a chord entirely consonant.

——— PERIOD, a termination satisfactory and agreeable to the ear.

——— TIME, a threefold time, in which the twofold note has the value of three whole notes.

PERFETTO, (*I.*) perfect, with regard to intervals, &c.

PERFORMER, a practical vocal or instrumental musician.

PERFIDIA. This word, borrowed from the Italians, signifies an affectation of doing always the same thing, following the same style.

PERIELESIS, a term formerly used in church music, signifying the interposition of one or more notes in the intonation, to indicate the approach of the final, and apprise the choir that they were to take up the theme.

PERIOD, PERIODE, (*I.*) PERIODE, (*F.*) } a complete musical sentence containing several members.

PERIODENBAU, (*G.*) the construction of musical periods.

PESANTE, (*I.*) with importance and weight, impressively.

PETITE MESURE A DEUX TEMS, (*F.*) $\frac{2}{4}$ time.

PETIT CHŒUR, (*F.*) a sacred composition in three parts.

PETITS PIECES, (*F.*) little pieces, short and easy compositions.

——— RIENS, light, trifling compositions.

PETTEIA, (*Gk.*) a name given by the ancients to the art of ascertaining the sounds which ought, or ought not, to be used; those which should be introduced, and those with which the strain should conclude.

PEU, (*F.*) a little.

PEZZE, (*I. Pl.*) fragments, select detached pieces of music.

PEZZI DI BRAVURA, pieces containing bold, spirited passages.

PHILŒLIA, a hymn sung by the ancient Greeks in honor of Apollo.

PHONICS, the art of treating musical sounds, either singly or in combination.

PHONASCE, (*Gk.*) name given by the ancients to those who taught the management of the voice.

PHORBEIA, (*Gk.*) a bandage. See *Capistrum.*

PHORMINX, (*Gk.*) a stringed instrument of remote antiquity, similar to the cithera, or lyre, but of superior tone and power.

PHOTINX, an ancient instrument resembling a flute.

PHRASE, an incomplete musical idea, generally occupying two bars, or at most three.

——— MANQUEES, (*F.*) imperfect and unsymmetrical passages introduced by injudicious composers, by which the melody is mained.

PHRYGIAN, the name of one of the ancient modes.

PHTONGOS, a sound or tone.

PIACERE, *a*, PIACEVOLE, PIACEVOLEMENTE, PIACEVOLEZZA, *con*, (*I.*) agreeably, with a gay and graceful expression.

PIANGENDO, PIANGEVOLE, PIANGEVOLMENTE, (*I.*) despondingly, plaintively, dolefully.

PIANISSIMO, or PP., (*I.*) extremely soft.

PIANO, (*I.*) soft. This word expresses a very slight degree of intensity; the opposite of *forte*.

——— PIANO, or PIU PIANO, (*I.*) more soft, or very soft.

——— A QUEUE, (*F.*) a horizontal grand piano-forte.

——— CARRE, (*F.*) a square piano.

——— FORTE SCHOOL, an extensive and complete method for the piano-forte.

——————— SCORE, a score in which the orchestral accompaniments are compressed into a piano-forte part; a vocal score.

PIANOGRAPHE, a highly ingenious machine, invented by M. Guerin, which, on being attached to the piano-forte, indicates, on paper prepared for the purpose, any thing played by the pianist.

PIATTI, (*I. Pl.*) the cymbals.

PIB-CORN, name given by the Welsh to a wind instrument, consisting of a wooden pipe with holes at the sides and a horn at each end.

PICCIOLO, PICCOLO, (*I.*) small; as, *flauto piccolo*, a small or octave flute.

PICHETTATO, (*I.*) } struck, intonated with vehemence.
PIQUE, (*F.*) }

PIEDS, (*F.*) the feet; as, *avec les pieds*, with the feet, in organ playing.

PIENA, (*I.*) full; as, *à piena orchestra*, for a full orchestra.

PIENO, (*I.*) full.

PIENAMENTE, fully.

PIETOSAMENTE, PIETOSO, (*I.*) with pity, compassionately.

PIFFERO, (*I.*) a fife.

PIPE. The pipe was one of the first of musical instruments. It is a tube formed of a reed, or of wood or metal.

PIPER, a performer on a pipe.

PIPES OF PAN, a wind instrument consisting of a range of pipes bound together, side by side, and gradually lessening, with respect to each other, in length and diameter.

PITCH, the acuteness or gravity of any particular sound, or the tuning of any instrument.

———PIPE, an instrument to ascertain the pitch of a key.

PITTORICO, embellished.

PIU, (*I.*) an adverb of augmentation; as,

—— FORTE, louder.

—— LENTO, slower.

—— MOSSO, with increased action.

—— PIANO, softer.

—— PRESTO, quicker.

—— TOSTO, (*I.*) rather; as,

———— ALLEGRO, rather quick.

PIVA, (*I.*) a bagpipe.

PIZZACANDO, PIZZICATO or PIZZ., (*I.*) in violin or violoncello music, is applied to notes which are to be twitched with the finger, instead of being played with the bow.

PLACIDO, calm and quiet.

PLACIDAMENTE, (*I.*) with placidity, quietly.

PLAGAL, the name applied to those church modes whose melody was confined within the limits of the dominant and its octave.

———CADENCE, the triad on the key-note preceded by that on the subdominant.

PLAIN CHANT, (*F.*) plain song or chant.

——— SONG, the old ecclesiastical chant without those harmonic appendages with which it has since been enriched.

PLANTIVO, (*I.*) expressively, plaintively.

PLAQUE, (*F.*) truck at once, in speaking of chords.

PLASMA, (*Gk.*) a term of the ancients, signifying a florid and a soft and delicate modulation of the voice.

PLAYERS ON HIGH AND LOW INSTRUMENTS, a title assumed by the French minstrels of the fourteenth century, when the laws of counterpoint were forming, and began to give exercise to bass and treble instruments in concert.

PLECTRUM, a piece of quill or ivory, used to twitch the strings of the mandoline, &c., instead of the fingers.

PLEIN JEU, (*F.*) full organ.

PLICA, name formerly given to a kind of ligature used in the old music, as a sign of hesitation or pause.

PLURITONE, any combination of musical sounds.

PLUS, (*F.*) more; as, *plus animé*, with greater animation.

PNEUMATIC, a word appropriated to wind instruments in general.

POCHETTE, (*F.*) a kit or small violin used by dancing masters.

POCHETTINO, POCHETTO, (*I.*) a very little; more or less, as the case may be; as, *ritard un pochettino*, slacken the time a little.

POCO, (*I.*) a little.

——— ANIMATO, (*I.*) a little more animated.

——— ADAGIO, a little slow.

——— MENO, somewhat less.

——— PIANO, somewhat soft.

——— PIU, somewhat more.

————— MOSSO, a little faster.

——— PRESTO, rather quick.

——— A POCO, (*I.*) by degrees, gradually.

——————— CRESCENDO, louder and louder, by degrees.

——————— DIMINUENDO, softer and softer by degrees.

POGGIATO, (*I.*) dwelt on, struck impressively.

POI, (*I.*) then; as, *adagio, poi allegro*, slow, then quick.

POINT, (*F.*) a dot.

——— D'ORGUE, (*F.*) a cadenza; also, a long holding-note in the bass, accompanied by various harmonies.

POINTEE, (*F.*) dotted; as, *blanche pointée*, a dotted minim.

POLACCA, (*I.*) a Polish dance in $\frac{3}{4}$ time, in which an emphasis is laid on the first unaccented part of the measure.

PÓLIPHANT, a stringed instrument.

POLONAISE, POLONOISE, (*F.*) a word synonymous with polacca. See *Polacca*.

POLKA, a rather quick Bohemian dance in $\frac{2}{4}$ time.

POLYCEPHALE, an air in ancient Greek music, performed by flutes, in honor of Apollo.

POLYMNASTIC, an ancient instrument of the flute kind.

POLYMORPHOUS, of many forms; an epithet generally applied to canons.

POLYPHONIA, (*Gk.*) a combination of many sounds.

POLYPHONIC, (*Gk.*) all compositions consisting of a plurality of parts, but generally confined to instrumental music, as concertos, overtures, &c.

POLYPLECTRUM, an instrument invented by Guido. So called from its strings being agitated by a number of quills.

POLYODIA, (*Gk.*) a musical composition.

POLYODIE, several parts in harmony.

POLYTHRONGUM, an instrument of many strings.

POMPOSO, (*I.*) in a grand and pompous manner.

PONTICELLO, (*I.*) the bridge of the violin or violoncello.

PONCTUATION MUSICALE, (*F.*) musical punctuation or phrasing.

PORRECTUS, one of the ten notes of the ancients.

PORTAMENTE DI VOCE, (*I.*) carrying the voice.

PORTANDO LA VOCE, (*I.*) sustaining the voice.

PORTAMENTO, (*I.*) the manner of sustaining and conducting the voice; a gliding from one note to another.

PORTAR LA VOCE, (*I.*)
PORTER LA VOIX, (*F.*) } to sustain the voice.

PORT-DE-VOIX, (*F.*) an appoggiatura.

PORTÉE, (*F.*) the stave on which the notes are written.

POSATO, (*I.*) quietly, steadily.

POSAUNE, (*G.*) the trombone.

POSITION, (*F.*) a position, or shift, on the violin, tenor, or violoncello.

POSITIF, (*F.*)
POSITIV, (*G.*) } the choir organ.

POSSIBILE, (*I.*) possible; as, *il più forte possibile*, as loud as possible.

POST-HORN, (*G.*) a sort of bugle; also, a movement suited to and imitating the notes of such an instrument.

POT POURRI, (*F.*) a capriccio or fantasia on favorite airs.

POUR, (*F.*) for.

—— **LA PREMIERE FOIS**, (*F.*) at the end of a strain, signifies that the passage over which it is placed is to be omitted in a repetition of that strain.

POULE, (*F.*) one of the movements of the quadrille.

POUSSÉ, (*F.*) in violin or violoncello music this term is used to indicate an up bow.

PRÆSCLÆ, females who sang dirges over the dead.

PRALL-TRILLER, (*G.*) a transient shake marked thus, ∿

PRATICO, (*I.*) practical.

PRECENTOR, the leader of the choir.

PRECETTORE MUSICO, a teacher of music.

PRECIPITAMENTE, PRECIPITATO, PRECIPITAZIONE, *con*, **PRECIPITOSO**, (*I.*) in a hurried manner.

PRECIPITE, (*F.*) hurried, accelerated.

PRECISIONE, (*I.*) with precision, exactitude.

PREGHIERA, (*I.*) a prayer.

PRELUDE, **PRELUDIO**, (*I.*) **PRELUDIUM**, (*L.*) } a short introductory and generally extemporaneous performance.

PREMIERE, (*F.*) first; as, *premiere fois*, first time.

PREPARATION, a term used by theorists to indicate that, in harmony, certain dissonant notes can only be employed with propriety when they have formed an integral part of the previous chord, and are continued on into the following chord.

PREPARED. See *Preparation*.

——— **DISCORD**, that discord the discordant note of which has been heard in a concord.

——— **SHAKE**, a shake preceded by ornamental notes.

PREPARAZIONE, (*I.*) the preparation of a dissonance.

PRESTAMENTE, (*I.*) hastily, rapidly.

PRESTEZZA, *con*, (*I.*) with haste and vivacity.

PRESTISSIMO, (*I.*) the superlative of *presto*; exceedingly quick.

PRESTO, (*I.*) extremely quick.

PRIMA BUFFA, (*I.*) the principal female performer in the Italian comic opera.

——— **DONNA**, (*I.*) the principal female singer in the Italian serious opera.

——— **VISTA**, (*I.*) at first sight.

——— **VOLTA**, (*I.*) the first time.

PRIME CANTANTE, in an opera, the first male singer.

PRIMO, (*I.*) first; as, *primo tempo*, return to the original time.

——— **BUFFO**, (*I.*) first comic male singer.

PRIMO MUSICO, (*I.*) first male singer in the serious or tragic opera.

——— TEMPO, at the point at which it is placed, renew the original time.

PRIMITIVE CHORD, that chord the lowest note of which is of the same literal denomination as the fundamental bass of the harmony.

PRINCIPAL, one of the most important stops in an organ. It is generally made of metal, runs throughout the whole compass of the key-board, and is tuned an octave above the diapasons.

PRINCIPALE, (*I.*) principal; as, *violino principale*, the principal violin.

PRINCIPALMENTE, (*I.*) principally.

PRINCIPIANTE, (*I.*) a beginner.

PROBE, (*G.*)
PROVA, (*I.*) } a rehearsal.

PROCELLA, a composition descriptive of a thunder storm.

PRODUCENTE, (*I.*) fifth tone of the scale.

PROFESSORE DI MUSICA, one who makes music his chief business.

PROGRAMMA, symphonies which form descriptive music.

PROGRESSIVE NOTES, those notes which succeed each other by those degrees the settled order of which constitutes the key of the composition, or the passage in which they occur.

PROHIBITO, forbidden, or not proper or according to just rule.

PROLATION, a method used in the old music of determining the power of semibreves and minims.

PROLONGED SHAKE, a shake which can be opened or closed at pleasure.

PRONTO, readily, quick, without loss of time.

PRONUNZIARE, (*I.*) to pronounce.

PROPE, near.

PROPOSTA, (*I.*) the subject of a fugue.

PROPORTION, the ratio which two terms bear to each other upon comparison.

PROSÆ, certain hymns used in the Romish church, consisting of rhyme without measure.

PROSCORDA, (*Gk.*) an instrumental accompaniment to ancient vocal music.

PROSLAMBANOMENOS, (*Gk.*) the name given to the lowest note in the Greek system, equivalent to our A.

PROSODIA, (*Gk.*) a sacred song or hymn, sung by the ancients in honor of their gods.

PROSODIAC, (*Gk.*) a Grecian air in honor of Mars.

PROSODY, the name of a melody sung by the Greeks at the entrance of sacrifices.

PROTESIS, a certain pause in ancient Greek music.

PROTRACTED MODULATION, that modulation which, before passing to its natural harmony, moves to an intermediate one.

PROTOPSALTES, the name of one of the principal singers in the patriarchal church of Constantinople.

PSALM, a sacred song.

PSALMODY ISLAND, an island in France, which had its name from a monastery founded there about the end of the fourteenth century, the constitution of which enjoined the preserving of a perpetual psalmody. See *Laus Perennis.*

PSALTERY, a ten-stringed instrument of the Hebrews.

PSALTRIÆ, females who sang at public feasts and banquets

PSAUME, (*F.*) psalm, a sacred song.

PUNKT, (*G.*) a dot.

PULSATILE, a term applied to such instruments as are made to sound by being struck upon, as a drum, a tambourine, &c.

PUNKTIRTE NOTEN, (*G.*) dotted notes.

PUNTA, (*I.*) the point; as, *colla punta dell' arco,* with the point or tip of the bow.

PUNTATO, (*I.*) pointed, detached.

PUNTO, (*I.*) dot or point.

——— PER PUNTO, (*I.*) note for note.

PUPITRE, (*F.*) a music desk.

PYKNOS, (*Gk.*) two of the genera of music, the chromatic and enharmonic.

PYRRHICS, ancient military dances in which the dancers were armed; also, a succession of two short notes.

Q.

QUADRICINIUM, a composition in four parts.

QUADRILLE, (*F.*) a French dance, or, rather, a set of five conseo utive dance movements, called *le pantalon, la poule, l'ete, la trenise ou la pastourelle, la finale.*

QUADRUPLE, fourfold.

——— COUNTERPOINT, counterpoint in four parts, all of which are invertible.

——— CROCHE, (*F.*) a semidemisemiquaver.

QUADRIVUM, the general name, in the ninth and tenth centuries, for the four sciences, music, arithmetic, geometry, and astronomy.

QUANTITY. This word, when applied to music, does not signify the number of the notes, but their relative duration. It is from the quantity as much as from the position of the notes that the beauty and expression of every melody proceed.

QUARTA, (*I.*)
QUARTE, (*F.* and *G.*) } the interval of a fourth.

QUARTA TONI, (*I.*)
QUARTE DU TON, (*F.*) } the subdominant, or fourth note of the scale.

QUARTER NOTE, a crotchet,

QUART DE TON, (*F.*)
QUARTER TONE,
QUARTO DI TUONO, (*I.*) } a small interval, which, in the mathematical theory of music, is found to exist between D♯ and E♭, G♯ and A♭, &c.

QUART-DE-SOUPIR, (*F.*)
QUARTO D'ASPETTO, (*I.*) } a semiquaver rest.

QUARTET,
QUARTETTO, (*I*) } a composition for four voices or instruments.

QUARTO, the fourth, the quarter note.

QUASI, (*I.*) in the manner or style of; as, *quasi allegretto*, like an allegretto.

——— ANDANTE, in the andante style.

——— PRESTO, rather fast.

QUATTRO, a piece for four hands or voices.

QUATUOR, (*F.*) four; same as quartet.

QUATRICOMA, a demisemiquaver.

QUART DE SON, (*F.*) a quarter tone.

QUAVER, a note equal in relative duration to one half of a crotchet, or one quarter of a minim in the same movement.

——— REST, an eighth rest.

QUERIMONIA, (*L.*) spiritual lamentation.

QUEERSTRICHE, (*G.*) ledger lines.

QUESTO, (*I.*) this, or that.

QUEUE, (*F.*) the tailpiece of a violin, violoncello, tenor, &c.; the tail or stem used to indicate the duration of a note.

QUICKSTEP, a lively, spirited march, generally in $\frac{2}{4}$ time.

QUIETO, (*I.*) with calmness or repose, quietly.

QUILISMA, name of one of the ten notes used in the middle ages.

QUINTA, QUINTE, QUINTO, the interval of a fifth.

QUINTET, QUINTETTO, (*I.*) QUINTOR, (*F.*) a composition for five voices or instruments.

QUINTOIER, (*F.*) a term applied by the old French writers on music to a species of descant chiefly consisting of fifths.

QUINTADECIMA, (*I.*) fifteenth.

QUINQUE, (*L.*) five.

QUI TOLLIS, (*L.*) a movement of the Gloria.

QUODLIBET, a term sometimes applied to a certain species of composition written in a comic style.

QUONIAM TU SOLUS, (*L.*) part of the Gloria.

R.

R., or R. H., indicates the right hand in piano-forte music.

RABBIA, (*I.*) with rage, furiously.

RADDOLCENDO, RADDOLCENTE, (*I.*) with augmented softness.

RADDOPIATO, doubled, or compounded.

RADDOPPIAMENTO, (*I.*) REDOUBLEMENT, (*F.*) the doubling of an interval.

RADICAL BASS, the fundamental bass.

RAGGIONE, ratio, proportion.

RALLENTANDO, (*I.*) implies a gradual diminution in the speed of the movement, and a corresponding decrease in the quantity of tone.

RANZ DES VACHES, (*F.*) airs played upon their pipes by the Swiss herdsmen, to assemble their herds and keep them together on their return home.

RAPIDAMENTE, RAPIDITA, *con*, RAPIDO, (*I.*) rapidly, with rapidity.

RAPPEL, (*F.*) in imitation of a bird.

RATTENENDO, (*I.*) restraining or holding back the time.

RAVVIVANDO, (*I.*) reviving, reanimating, accelerating; as, *ravvivando il tempo*, animating or quickening the time.

RE, a syllable applied, in solfaing, to the note D.

REALE. *A quatro voce reale*, in four, or for four parts, vocal or instrumental.

REBEC, a Moorish instrument with two strings, to which the Spaniards added a third.

RECHEAT, the name by which huntsmen designate those sounds which are played on the horn to recall the hounds from a false scent.

RECHT, (*G.*) right; as, *rechte hand*, the right hand.

RECITANDO, (*I.*) in the style of recitation; declamatory.

RECITANTE, (*I.*) in the style of a recitative.

RECITATIF, (*F.*) } a recitative.
RECITARE, }

RECITATIVE, a species of musical recitation. It was first introduced in the year 1660, at Rome.

RECITATIVO, (*I.*) a recitative or musical declamation.

——— PARLANTE, in a speaking manner.

——— SECCO, (*I.*) unaccompanied recitative.

——— STROMENTATO, (*I.*) recitative accompanied by the orchestra.

RECLAME, (*F.*) a vocal performance resembling a bird's song.

RECLAMER, (*F.*) one who sings a reclame.

RECORDER, an old wind instrument somewhat resembling a flute, but of smaller bore and shriller tone.

RECTE, (*L.*) forwards.

RECTOR CHORI, (*L.*) the leader of a choir.

REDITTA, (*I.*) a term denoting that the strain or passage over which it is written is to be repeated.

REDOUBLED, an epithet applied to any simple interval carried into its octave; as, the thirteenth, composed of a sixth and octave, is a redoubled sixth; and the fifteenth, containing two octaves, is a redoubled octave.

REEDS, thin pieces of wood which form the mouthpiece of the hautboy, clarinet, and bassoon.

REEL, a sprightly Scotch dance, the accompanying tune of which is in common time.

REFRAIN, (*F.*) an old term for the burden of a song.

REGINA CŒLI, (*L.*) a hymn to the Virgin.

REGISTER, the compass of a voice or instrument; also, an organ stop of any species.

REGLE, (*F.*)
REGOLA, (*I.*) } a rule or precept for composition or performance.

REGLE DE L'OCTAVE, (*F.*) the rule of the octave, showing the manner of harmonizing the scale taken as a bass.

REGULAR MOTION, similar motion.

REHEARSAL, a preparatory performance.

RELATION, that connection which any two sounds have with one another in respect of the interval which they form.

RELATIVE, those chords, modes, or keys, which, by reason of affinity and identity of some of their component parts, admit of an easy and natural transition from one to the other.

——— **KEYS**, those keys which only differ by having in their scales one flat or sharp more or less, or which have the very same signatures.

RELIGIOSAMENTE, RELIGIOSO, (*I.*) in a solemn style.

REMISSIO, the act of the voice when it descends from a high note to a low one; the reverse of *intentio*.

RENVERSEMENT, (*F.*) an inversion.

RENVOI, (*F.*) a mark of repetition.

RÉPÉTITION, (*F.*) a rehearsal.

REPETIZIONE, (*I.*) repetition; as, *senza repetizione*, without repetition.

REPETATUR, let it be repeated.

REPLICA, (*I.*) repetition; as, *senza replica*, without repeating; *con replica*, with repetition.

REPERCUSSION, a frequent repetition of the same sound.

REPLICATO, (*I.*) repeated.

RÉPONSE, (*F.*) the answer of a fugue.

REPRISE, (*F.*) a repetition or return to some preceding part.

——— **D'UN OPERA**, (*F.*) the representation of an opera which has not been given for some time.

REQUIEM, (*L.*) a musical service for the dead.

RESOLUTION, the concord which necessarily follows a preceding discord is called its resolution.

RESOLUZIONE, (*I.*) resolution.

RESOLVED, the result of resolution.

RESONANCE, a prolongation or reflection of any sound.

RESPONSAY, in church music, an anthem of any kind, in which the choir and the people sing by turns.

RESPIRO, (*I.*) a semiquaver rest.

RESTS, the characters which indicate silence in music.

RETARDATION, the continuation of one or more notes of a chord into the following chord.

RETRO, (*L.*) backward; the reverse of *recte*.

RETROGRADO, (*I.*) in retrograde movement.

RETTO, (*I.*) direct; as, *moto retto*, direct or similar motion

RHAPSODIE, (*F.*) a rhapsody, a capriccio.

RHAPSODISTS, or RHAPSODI, (*Gk.*) persons among the ancients whose profession it was to sing or recite the verses of Homer, and other celebrated poets.

RHYTHM, the theory of musical cadence, as applied to melody.

RHYTHMICS, rhythmical forms and delineations.

RHYTHMICAL, relating to rhythm.

RHYTHMICA, a branch of ancient music which regulated the rhythm.

RHYTHMOPŒIA, one of the ancient musical faculties, as they were called, which prescribed rules for rhythm.

RICERCARI, (*I. Pl.*) difficult exercises for the voice or for some instrument.

RICERCATA, (*I.*) a fugue replete with contrapuntal artifices.

RICORDANZA, (*I.*) with recollection, remembrance.

RIDOTTO, (*I.*) adapted, arranged; also, an entertainment consisting of singing and dancing.

RIDURE. See *Ridotto*.

RIFFIORIMENTI, (*I. Pl.*) extemporaneous embellishments.

RIFLETTANDO, a reflective air to be assumed.

RIGADOON, an antiquated French dance in triple time.

RIGORE, in the most exact time.

RIGOLS, an old instrument consisting of several sticks by the side of each other, but separated by beads.

RINFORZANDO, RINFORZATO, RINFORZO, RINF. or RF. *abb.*, (*I.*) with additional tone and emphasis.

RIPIENO, (*I.*) a term applied to such parts, in concerted music, as are intended to fill up and augment the effect of the *tutti*, or full chorus of voices or instruments.

RIPOSTA, repeat.

RIPRESA, (*I.*) a mark of repetition.

RISOLUMENTE, RISOLUTO, RISOLUZIONE, *con*, (*I.*) in a bold, decided style.

RISOLUTISSIMO, (*I.*) with extreme resolution.

RISOLUZIONE, (*I.*) the resolution of a discord.

RISPOSTA, (*I.*) the answer of a fugue.

RISVEGLIATO, (*I.*) with much animation.

RISVEGLIARE, (*I.*) to reanimate the execution.

RITARDANDO, RITARDATO, (*I.*) implies a gradual retarding or slackening of the time, with a corresponding diminution in point of tone.

RITARDO, (*I.*) a retardation.

RITENENDO, (*I.*) holding back in the time.

RITENENTE, RITENUTO, (*I.*) slackening the time. The effect differs from the *ritardando* by being done at once, while the other is effected by degrees.

RITORNELLO, (*I.*) a short symphony or introduction to an air, as also the symphonies between the members or periods of the air. The same term is applied also to the *tutti* parts, introductory to, and between the solos of a concerto.

RIVOLGIMENTO, (*I.*) the inversion of the parts in double counterpoint.

RIVERSA, the opposite.

RIVESCIO, the reverse.

RIVOLTATO, (*I.*) inverted.

RIVOLTO, (*I.*) an inversion.

ROHR, (*G.*) a reed.

ROHRWERK, (*G.*) reed-work, the reed stops taken collectively.

ROLLO, (*I.*)
ROLLANDO, (*I.*)
ROULEMENT, (*F.*) } the roll on the drum and tambourine.

ROMANCE, (*F.*)
ROMANZA, (*I.*) } a short lyric tale, set to music, or a simple and elegant melody suitable to such words.

ROMANESQUE, (*F.*) a dance tune, called also *galliard*.

RÖMISCHE GESANG, (*G.*) the plain chant of the Catholic service.

RONDE, (*F.*) a semibreve.

RONDEAU, (*F.*) } a composition of several strains or members,
RONDO, (*I.*) } at the end of each of which the first part or subject is repeated.

RONDILETTA, RONDINETTO, RONDINO, RONDOLETTO, (*I.*) a short rondo.

ROOT, the fundamental note of any chord.

ROSALIA, (*I.*) the repetition of a passage several times over, each time ascending one degree.

ROTE, the old name of the hurdy-gurdy.

ROTONDO, (*I.*) round or full, as regards tone.

ROULADE, (*F.*) a division or rapid flight of notes.

ROULEMENS, (*F.*) a term applied to all kinds of rapid passages.

ROUND, a sort of canon in the unison.

ROUNDELAY, a sort of antique poem, in various parts of which a return is made to the first verse or couplet; a poetical rondo.

ROVESCIO, (*I.*) inverted, reverted.

RUBATO, (*I.*) robbed, borrowed. The terms *tempo rubato* are applied to a style of performance in which some notes are held longer than their legitimate time, while others are curtailed of their proportionate duration, in order that, on the whole, the aggregate value of the bar may not be disturbed.

RÜCKUNG, (*G.*) syncopation.

RUHEPUNCT, (*G.*) a point of repose in melody, a cadence.

RUSSE, (*F.*) Russian; as, *à la Russe*, in the Russian style.

S.

SACKBUT, an old-fashioned instrument, resembling a trombone.

SACRIST, a person employed in a cathedral to copy music and have charge of the books.

SAGGIO, (*I.*) an essay.

SAITE, (*G.*) a string of a musical instrument.

SAITENHALTER, (*G.*) the tailpiece of a violin, tenor, &c.

SALII, (*L.*) the name given by the Romans to the young men, twelve in number, who were appointed to sing hymns in praise of the god of war.

SALMO, (*I.*) a psalm or psalm tune.

SALMODIA, (*I.*) psalmody.

SALTANDO, (*I.*) proceeding by skips or bounds.

SALTERELLA. See *Sartarella.*

SALTERIO, SALTERO, (*I.*) a Psalter or book of psalms.

SALTO, (*I.*) a skip.

SALVE REGINA, (*L.*) a hymn addressed to the Virgin.

SAMBUCA, (*Gk.*) an ancient stringed instrument.

SAMBUCUS, (*Gk.*) an ancient wind instrument.

SAMPUNIA, a pneumatic instrument used by the ancient Hebrews, resembling the modern bagpipe.

SANCTUS, (*L.*) a part of the mass in the Catholic service.

SANFT, (*G.*) soft; as, *mit sanften stimmen*, with soft stops, in organ music.

SÄNGER, (*G.*) a singer.

SANS, (*F.*) without; as, *sans pedales*, without the pedals, in organ playing.

SARABANDA, (*I.*) }
SARABANDE, (*F.*) } a saraband, an antique slow dance tune.

SARTARELLA, SARTARELLO, (*I.*) a Neapolitan dance.

SATTEL, (*G.*) the nut of a violin finger-board, &c.

SBARRA DOPPIA, (*I.*) a double bar.

SCALA, (*I.*) a scale or gamut.

——— CHROMATIC, the chromatic scale.

SCALD, among the northern nations, implies a bard or poet musician.

SCANELLO, SCAGNELLO, SCANNETTO, (*I.*) name given by the Italians to the bridge of a violin, violoncello, &c.

SCAVEZZA, (*I.*) divisions within the compass of the sixth.

SCENA, (*I.*) a scene or portion of an opera. An act is generally composed of several scenes.

——— DA CAMERA, (*I.*) a term applied by the Italians to all vocal compositions not designed for the church or theatre.

SCHEME, a term used in ancient music to express the varieties arising from the different positions of tones and semitones in a consonance.

SCHERZATO, light and playful.

SCHERZANDO, SCHERZANTE, SCHERZO, SCHERZEVOLMENTE, SCHERZOSAMENTE, SCHERZOSO, SCHERZ., *abb.*, (*I.*) in a light, playful, and sportive manner.

SCHERZANDISSIMO, (*I.*) in an exceedingly playful style.

SCHISMA, in ancient music, a small interval equal to the half of a comma, or the eighteenth part of a tone.

SCHŒNION, (*Gk.*) a scientific air composed for flutes.

SCHOTTISCHE, (*G.*) the name given to a rather slow modern dance in $\frac{2}{4}$ time.

SCHLEIFEZEICHEN, (*G.*) a slur.

SCHUSTERFLECK, (*G.*) synonymous with *Rosalia.* See that word.

SCHLÜSSEL, (*G.*) the clef.

SCHNARRPFEIFEN, (*G.*) reed work, reed stops.

SCHNELL WALZER, (*G.*) quick waltzes.

SCHREIBART, (*G.*) style.

SCHULE, (*G.*) a school or method for learning any instrument, &c.

SCHWACH, (*G.*) piano, or soft.

SCHWEIGE, (*G.*) a rest.

SCIALUMO, (*F.*) in clarinet music, signifying that the notes are to be played an octave lower than written.

SCIOLTAMENTE, (*I.*) with freedom and agility.

SCIOLTO, (*I.*) with freedom and boldness.

SCOLARO, (*I.*) a scholar.

SCOLIA, (*Gk.*) name given by the ancients to songs in general, but more especially to those of a festive kind.

SCOLIUM, (*Gk.*) a festive song.

SCORDATO, out of tune.

SCORE, a complete and orderly assemblage, in one view, of the parts of a vocal or instrumental composition.

SCORING, the forming of a score, by collecting and properly arranging the detached parts of a composition.

SCOTCH SCALE, a scale differing from that of the other nations of Europe by its omission of the fourth and seventh; a peculiarity from which all the genuine Scottish melodies derive their national and distinguished character.

SCOZZESE, *alla*, (*I.*) in the style of Scotch music.

SDEGNO, *con*, SDEGNOZAMENTE, SDEGNOZO, (*I.*) in a fiery and indignant style.

SDRUCCIOLARE, (*I.*) the gliding of the nails up and down the keys of the piano-forte.

SDRUCCIOLATO, (*I.*) sliding the nail of the first finger over the keys, as in the one-fingered waltz of Mozart.

SEC, (*F.*)
SECCO, (*I.*) } in a dry or unornamented manner.

SECHZENTHEIL NOTE, (*G.*) a semiquaver.

SECONDE, (*F.*) second; as, *seconde fois*, second time.

SECONDA, SECONDO, (*I.*) the second.

SECULAR MUSIC, all music not designed for religious purposes.

SECULARS, unordained officiates of any cathedral or chapel, whose functions are confined to the vocal department of the choir.

SECUNDE, (*G.*) the interval of a second.

SEGNO, or 𝄋, (*I.*) a sign; as, *al segno*, return to the sign; *dal segno*, repeat from the sign.

SEGUENDO, SEGUENTE, (*I.*) following.

SEGUE, SEGUITO, (*I.*) now follows, or as follows. Examples; *segue il coro*, the chorus follows; *segue la finale*, the finale now follows. It is also used in the sense of in similar, or like manner, to show that a subsequent passage is to be played like that which precedes it.

SEGUIDILLA, a favorite Spanish dance in simple triple time.

SEI, six.

SEITENBEWEGUNG, (*G.*) oblique motion.

SEIZIEME DE SOUPIR, (*F.*) a semidemisemiquaver rest.

SEMI, (*L.*) half; as, *semitone*, half a tone, &c.

SEMIBREVE, a long note equal to two minims or four crotchets, &c.

SEMICON, an ancient instrument of thirty-five strings.

SEMICHORUS, a chorus to be sung by only a portion of the voices.

SEMICHROMA, (*I.*) a semiquaver.

SEMIDEMISEMIQUAVER, a quadruple quaver, or a note having four tails, equal in duration to one half of a demisemiquaver.

SEMIDIAPENTE, (*L.*) the diminished or imperfect fifth.

SEMIDIAPASON, an octave diminished by a minor semitone.

SEMIDIATESSERON, a false fifth.

SEMIDITONE, (*L.*) the minor third.

SEMIFUSA, (*L.*) the ancient name for a semiquaver.

SEMIMINIMA, (*L.*) a crotchet.

SEMITONE, a half tone.

SEMITONICS, intervals consisting of half tones.

SEMITONIUM MODI, (*L.*) the leading note.

SEMITUONO, (*I.*) a semitone.

SEMPLICE, SEMPLICEMENTE, SEMPLICITA, *con*, (*I.*) with simplicity, artlessly.

SEMPRE, (*I.*) always; *sempre staccato,* always staccato or detached; *sempre forte,* always loud; *sempre più forte,* continually increasing in force.

——— **CON FORZA,** perform loud throughout.

SENSIBILE, SENSIBILITA, *con,* (*I.*) with sensibility and feeling.

SENSIBLE, (*F.*) the leading note or major seventh of the scale.

SENTIMENTALE, SENTIMENTO, *con,* (*I.*) with feeling and sentiment.

SENZA, (*I.*) without; as, *senza organo,* without the organ; *senza replica,* without repetition.

——— **RIGORE,** (*I.*) not in strict time; in some degree *ad libitum.*

SEPTETTO, (*I.*) a septet, or piece for seven instruments.

SEPTENARY, a scale in which the eighth tone is omitted.

SEPTET, SEPTUOR, a composition for seven voices or instruments.

SEPTIEME, (*F.*) }
SEPTIME, (*G.*) } the interval of a seventh.

SEQUENCE, a succession of similar chords or intervals.

SEQUENTIA, (*L.*) hymns used in the Romish church, so called because, though in their composition rhyme is adhered to, the laws of measure and quantity are neglected. Of this kind is the Stabat Mater.

SEGUENZA, (*I.*) a sequence of similar intervals or chords.

SESQUALTRA, SESQUIALTRA, an organ stop, of a shrill, noisy quality of tone, consisting of several ranks of pipes tuned in thirds, fifths, or octaves.

SERBANO, (*I.*) the serpent, a bass wind instrument, somewhat in that form.

SERENADE, a concert performed at night, under the windows of the person to be entertained.

SERENATA, (*I.*) a vocal composition on an amorous subject.

SERIA, (*I.*) serious; as, *opera seria,* a serious or tragic opera.

SERIOSO, (*I.*) in a grave and serious style.

SERPEGGIANDO, (*I.*) sliding, creeping gently onwards.

SERPENT, a military wind instrument, of a deep pitch and of a coarse quality of tone.

SERPENTONO, (*I.*) serpent.

SERVICE, certain portions of the Protestant ritual when set to music.

SERVI SYMPHONIACI, (*L.*) among the Romans, a band of musicians kept by a person of rank, for the amusement of himself or guests.

SESQUI, a Latin particle signifying a whole and a half.

SESQUITERTIA, a musical ratio, when it is as four to three.

SESQUITONE, a minor third, or an interval consisting of three semitones.

SESQUIALTERA, an organ stop composed of several ranks of pipes.

SESTA, (*I.*) a sixth.

SESTETTO, (*I.*) } a vocal or instrumental composition in six parts.
SESTET, }

SETTIMA, (*I.*) a seventh.

SETZART, (*G.*) style of composition.

SETZKUNST, (*G.*) the art of musical composition.

SEVENTH, an interval formed of seven sounds.

SEVERAMENTE, SEVERITA, *con*, (*I.*) in a strict and severe style.

SEXTA PARS, (*L.*) four parts, being the number to which church compositions were limited during the fifteenth century.

SEXTE, (*G.*) the interval of a sixth.

SEXTUOR, a composition for six voices or instruments.

SEXTUPLE, name formerly given to what is now called *compound common time.*

SFORZANDO, SFORZATO, (*I.*) implies that a particular note is to be played with emphasis and force.

SFUGGITO, (*I.*) avoided; as, *cadenza sfuggita*, an avoided (i. e., a broken) cadence.

SHAKE, an embellishment consisting of the alternate reiteration of two notes comprehending an interval not greater than one whole tone, nor less than a semitone.

SHARP, a character, the power of which is to raise the note before which it is placed half a tone.

SHAWM, a wind instrument of the ancient Hebrews.

SHIFT, a change of the position of the hand along the finger-board of a violin, violoncello, &c., necessary to the execution.

SHORT OCTAVES, an appellation given to some of the lower octaves of an organ, because, from the omission of some of the intermediate notes, the extreme keys lie nearer to each other than those of the full octaves.

SHRILL, an epithet applied to those acute sounds which form the upper part of the scale of soprano voices and treble instruments.

SI, a syllable applied, in solfaing, to the note B.

SICILIANA, (*I.*) a movement of a slow, soothing, pastoral character, in $\frac{6}{8}$ time, resembling the dance peculiar to the peasantry of Sicily.

SIEGUE, SIEQUE, (*I.*) it follows; as, *siegue il menuetto*, the *menuetto* follows. When applied to a particular passage, it signifies that though it does not continue to be made out in the same form of notes in which it commenced, yet the same style of execution is to be preserved.

SIGNATURE, (*F.*) the signature, or name given to the aggregate of sharps or flats necessary to each key, and placed at the beginning of each stave.

SIGNE, (*F.*) the :S:, or direct.

SILENCE, (*F.*) a rest.

SIMI-CUM, (*Gk.*) an ancient instrument having thirty-five strings.

SIMILAR MOTION, that in which two or more parts always ascend or descend at the same time.

SIMILE, (*I.*) similarly, in like manner.

SIMPLE, a term applied to that counterpoint in which note is set against note, and which is called *simple*, in opposition to more elaborate composition, known as *figurative* counterpoint.

——— INTERVALS, such as do not exceed an octave.

——— SOUND, a pure, unmixed, single sound.

——— TIMES, those measures which contain but one principal accent; as, $\frac{2}{4}$, $\frac{3}{2}$, $\frac{3}{8}$, &c.

SINCOPA. See *Syncope*.

SINFONIA, (*I.*) } a symphony or orchestral composition in many
SINFONIE, (*G.*) } parts.

SINGHIOZZANDO, (*I.*) sobbingly.

SINGLE CHANT, a simple harmonized melody extending only to one verse of a psalm as sung in cathedrals, &c.

SINGSCHULE, (*G.*) a singing school.

SINGSTIMMEN, (*G. Pl.*) the voices, the vocal parts.

SINISTRA, SINISTRÆ, (*L.*) the left hand. By this name the Romans distinguished their left-handed flutes; those made for the right hand were called *dextræ*.

SINO, or SIN', (*I.*) as far as; as, *con fuoco sin' al fine*, with spirit to the end.

—— AL FINE, to the conclusion.

SI PIACE, perform as you choose, or omit if you think best.

— RADOPPIA IL TEMPO, time or movement to be increased one half.

— REPLICA, (*I.*) repeat.

— TACE, (*I.*) be silent.

SIGUES DES SILENCES, (*F.*) signs of rest.

SISTRUM, an ancient Egyptian instrument of percussion.

SIXTE, (*F.*) a sixth.

SIXTEENTH NOTE, a semiquaver, 

SIX POUR QUATRE, (*F.*) six notes meant to be played in the time of four, a sextuplet.

SIXTH, an interval comprising six degrees.

SKIPPING NOTES, notes which do not proceed by conjoint degrees, nor in any regular course, but lie at awkward and unexpected distances from each other.

SLEGATO, to separate or disconnect.

SLENTANDO, (*I.*) a gradual diminution in the time or speed of the movement.

SLUR, a curved line drawn over two or more notes to indicate that they must be smoothly connected.

SLURRING, performing in a smooth, gliding style.

SLIDE, two notes gradually rising or falling towards the principal note.

SMANICARE, (*I.*) to change the position of the hand on such instruments as the violin, guitar, &c.

SMANICANDO, the neck of an instrument.

SMANIOSO, (*I.*) with fury.

SMINUENDO, (*I.*) gradually diminishing the sound.

SMORFIOSO, (*I.*) in an affected manner.

SMORZANDO, SMORZATO, (*I.*) diminishing the sound, dying away by degrees.

SOAVE, (*I.*) softly, sweetly.

SOAVÁMENTE, (*I.*) with great sweetness.

SOECK-PIPE, name given by the ancient northern poets to the bagpipe.

SOGGETTO, (*I.*) a subject or theme.

SOL, a monosyllable applied by the Italians to G, the fifth sound of the diatonic scale or octave of C.

SOLENNEMENTE, (*I.*) solemnly.

SOLENNITA, (*I.*) with solemnity.

SOLFA, SOLFAING, the practice of solfeggi by means of the syllables Do, Re, Mi, Fa, Sol, La, Si, corresponding to the notes C, D, E, F, G, A, B.

SOLFEGE, (*F.*)
SOLFEGGI, (*I. Pl.*)
SOLFEGGIO, (*I.*) } exercises for the voice.

SOLFEGGIARE, SOLMIZARE, extemporaneous, to sing without text.

SOLFEGGIAMENTI, (*I.*) compositions intended as exercises for singing at sight.

SOLI, (*I. Pl.*) implies that two or more principal parts play or sing together; such parts, of course, are never doubled.

SOLITO, in the usual manner.

SOLLECITO, (*I.*) in an ardent, solicitous, and pensive style.

SOLMIZATION, the same as solfaing.

——— *a la Grec*, a species of solmization formerly practised, in which a strict adherence to the Greek system of tetrachords was observed.

SOLO, SOLA, (*I.*) alone; a composition, or even a passage for a single voice or instrument, with or without accompaniments.

SONATA, (*I.*)
SONATE, (*F.*) } a composition consisting of several movements, generally for a single principal instrument, with or without accompaniments.

SONATA DA CAMERA, a sonata designed for the chamber or parlor.

——— CHIESA, a sonata for church.

——— DI BRAVURA, a brave, bold style of sonata.

SONATINA, (*I.*)
SONATINE, (*F.*) } a short and easy sonata.

SONNET, a short poem of only fourteen lines.

SONETTO, sonnet.

SONG, a short lyric poem set to music. The ancients had the art of singing before they had that of writing, and their laws, as well as their histories, were sung long before they were inscribed.

SONI MOBILES, name by which the ancients distinguished the intermediary sounds of their tetrachords.

SONI STABILES, or SONI STANTES, the extremes of the Greek tetrachords.

SONORAMENTE, (*I.*)
SONORITA, *con*, (*I.*)
SONORITÉ, (*F.*)
} sonorously; with a full, vibrating kind of tone.

SONORE, (*F.*)
SONORO, (*I.*)
} sonorous, full toned.

SONOROUS, an epithet applied to whatever is capable of yielding sounds.

SONS, (*F.*) the name of the airs and lyric poems of the Provençal minstrels.

—— ETOUFFES, (*F.*) soft tones produced on the harp by checking the vibration of the strings.

—— HARMONIQUES, (*F. Pl.*) harmonic sounds or notes.

—— PLEINS, (*F. Pl.*) terms which often occur in flute music, and which indicate that the notes must be blown with a very full, round tone.

SOPRA, (*I.*) above; as, *come sopra*, as above; *contrapunto sopra il soggetto*, counterpoint above the subject.

SOPRANO, (*I.*) the highest species of female voice.

SOPRANI, plural of *soprano*.

SORDAMENTE, (*I.*) damped, muffled.

SORDINI, (*I. Pl.*) mutes; as, *con sordini*, with mutes, *senza sordini*, without mutes, on the violin, tenor, &c.

SORDINO, (*I.*) a mute or damper applied to the bridge of the violin, tenor, &c.

SOSPIRANDO, (*I.*) with apprehension, despondingly.

SOSPENSIONE, (*I.*) a suspension.

SOSPIRO, (*I.*) a crotchet rest.

SOSTENUTO, or SOST., (*I.*) sustained, continuous in regard to tone.

SOSTENENDO, (*I.*) an even degree of tone throughout.

SOTTO, (*I.*) under; as, *sotto il soggetto*, under the subject.

—— VOCE, (*I.*) in a soft or subdued manner, in an under tone.

SOUDELINE, (*F.*) a kind of musette or bagpipe.

SOUPIR, (*F.*) a crotchet rest.

SOUSDOMINANTE, (*F.*) the subdominant or fourth of the scale.

SOUSMEDIANTE, (*F.*) the submediant or sixth of the scale.

SOUSTONIQUE, (*F.*) the seventh of the scale or subtonic.

SOUVENIRS, (*F. Pl.*) recollections, reminiscences, keepsakes.

SPACES, the intervals between the lines of the staff.

SPAGNUOLA, (*I.*) the guitar.

SPALLA, the shoulder.

SPATIUM, the space.

SPAZIO, (*I.*) a space of the stave.

SPECIES, in ancient music, the subdivision of the genera.

SPIANATA, (*I. adjective,*) smooth; as, *voce spianata*, an even and sustained voice; drawn out, as when several notes are given to each syllable.

SPICCATO, (*I.*) This word indicates that every note must be played in a very distinct and detached manner.

SPIELEN, (*G.*) to play upon an instrument.

SPINET, SPINETTA, an old keyed instrument.

SPIRITO, *con*, SPIRITOSAMENTE, SPIRITOSO, (*I.*) with spirit, animation.

SPIRITUALE, (*I.*) sacred.

SPISSUS, thick, full, as of small or minute parts, as of intervals.

SPONDAULA, (*Gk.*) name given by the ancients to a performer on the flute.

SPONDEE, a musical foot consisting of two long notes.

SPONDEASMUS, the enharmonic genus when raised three dieses.

SPONDIASM, (*Gk.*) an alteration in the harmonic genus, by which a chord was elevated three dieses above its ordinary pitch.

STA, (*I.*) } as it stands.
STAT, (*L.*) }

STABAT MATER, (*L.*) a hymn on the crucifixion.

STACCATISSIMO, (*I.*) very detached.

STACCATO, (*I.*) This term implies that the notes are to be played distinct, short, and detached from one another by rests.

STAFF, or STAVE, lines on which notes are written.

STANGHETTA, (*I.*) a bar line.

STARK, (*G.*) forte, loud; as, *mit starken stimmen*, with loud stops, in organ playing.

STEG, (*G.*) the bridge of a violin, violoncello, &c.

STEM, the thin stroke which is drawn from the head of a note.

STENTATO, (*I.*) in a loud, bawling manner, for some particular effect.

STENTANDO, protracting, delaying.

STENTOROPHONIC TUBE, a speaking trumpet, so called from Stentor, the herald mentioned by Homer, who, as that author says, could call louder than fifty men. The Stentorophonic horn of Alexander the Great is said to have enabled him to give orders to his army at a distance of above twenty English miles.

STESSO, (*I.*) the same.

STHÉNOCHIRE, a machine for strengthening and imparting flexibility to the fingers, being a compound of the dactylion and the handguide.

STIBACCHIATO, (*I.*) dragging, relaxing in the time.

STICCATO, (*I.*) a musical instrument, the sounds of which are produced by striking on little bars of wood.

STILO, (*I.*) style, either of composition, or of performance.

——— DI RECITATIVO, (*I.*) a tedious, monotonous style of composition formerly much adopted in Italy.

STIMME, (*G.*) This word has various significations; as, the voice; the sound-post of a violin, &c.; a part in vocal or instrumental music; and a stop of an organ.

STIMMSTOCK, (*G.*) the sound-post of a violin, &c.

STINGUENDO, (*I.*) gradually diminishing the tone.

STOP, the pressure of the fingers on the strings of a violin, violoncello, &c.

——— OF AN ORGAN, a collection of pipes similar in tone and quality, which run through the whole, or a great part of the compass of the instrument. In a great organ the stops are numerous and multifarious, commonly comprising the following: —

Bassoon Stop, a reed stop, imitative of the instrument from which it derives its name.

Cremona Stop, a reed stop, in unison with the diapasons.

Cornet Stop, a stop consisting of five pipes to each note.

Clarion, or *Octave Trumpet Stop*, resembling the tone of the trumpet, but an octave higher than the trumpet stop.

Dulciana Stop, a stop of peculiar sweetness of tone, which it chiefly derives from the bodies of its pipes being longer and smaller than those of the pipes of the other stops.

Flute Stop, a stop imitative of the common flute or flageolet.

Fifteenth Stop, a stop which derives its name from its pitch, or scale, being fifteen notes above that of the diapason.

Hautboy Stop, a reed stop, having a tone in imitation of the hautboy.

Larigot Stop, or *Octave Twelfth*, a stop, the scale of which is an octave above the twelfth.

Mixture, or *Furniture Stop*, a stop comprising two or more ranks of pipes, shriller than those of the *Sesquialtera*.

Open Diapason Stop, a metallic stop, which commands the whole scale of the organ.

Principal Stop, a metallic stop, so called because holding, in point of pitch, the middle station between the diapason and fifteenth.

Stopt-Diapason Stop, so called from having its pipes stopped at the top with a wooden plug, by which it is tuned, and by which its notes are rendered soft and mellow.

Sesquialtera Stop, a mixed stop running through the scale of the instrument, and consisting of three, four, and sometimes five ranks of pipes, tuned in thirds, fifths, and eighths.

Tierce Stop, a stop tuned a major third higher than the fifteenth, and only employed in the full organ.

Trumpet Stop, so called because its tone is imitative of a trumpet. In large organs it generally extends through the whole compass.

Twelfth Stop, a metallic stop, so denominated from its being tuned twelve notes above the diapason.

Vox-humana Stop, a stop, the tone of which resembles the human voice.

STRAIN, a portion of a movement divided off by a double bar.

STRASCINANDO, STRASCINO, (*I.*) a grace chiefly vocal, and used in slow passages. It is a kind of drag, and consists of about eight or ten notes given in an unequal and descending motion.

STRASCINATO, (*I.*) relaxing in the movement.

STRATHSPEY, a lively Scotch dance in common time.

STRENG, (*G.*) strict, in relation to style.

STREPITOSAMENTE, (*I.*) with much noise and power.

STREPITO, *con*, STREPITOSO, (*I.*) in an impetuous, boisterous style; noisy manner.

STRETTO, (*I.*) a knot. This term is often met with in modern music towards the end of long movements, where it is used to indicate a considerable acceleration of the time. It is also used in fugue writing, to imply that the subject and answer begin much nearer to one another than at the commencement of the fugue.

STRICCIANDO, (*I.*) dragging in the time.

STRICHARTEN, (*G. Pl.*) different ways of bowing.

STRING, any wire, or preparation of sheep or catgut, used in musical instruments. The ancients originally strung their instruments with thongs of leather, but afterwards adopted various metals, including silver and gold.

STRINGED, an epithet applied to those instruments, the sonorous parts of which consist of strings.

STRINGENDO, (*I.*) accelerating the degree of movement.

STROFFA, (*I.*) strophe.

STROMENTI, (*I. Pl.*) musical instruments in general; as, *stromenti di vento*, wind instruments, &c.

STROPHICUS, one of the ten notes used in the middle ages.

STUDIO, (*I.*) a study or exercise for some particular instrument.

STUFE, (*G.*) a degree; as, *stufe der tonleiter*, a degree of the scale.

STYLE, that cast or manner in composition or performance on which the effect chiefly depends.

SUAVE, SUAVEMENTE, SUAVITA, *con*, (*I.*) with sweetness and delicacy of expression.

SUB, (*L.*) under, below.

SUBBASS, (*G.*) a stop or set of pipes belonging to the pedals.

SUBDOMINANT, the fourth note of the scale of any key.

SUBITAMENTE, SUBITO, (*I.*) quickly; as, *volti subito*, turn over quickly.

SUBJECT, the theme or text of a movement.

SUBMEDIANT, the sixth of the scale.

SUBSEMITONE, the semitone below the key note.

SUBSEMITONIUM MODI, (*L.*) the leading note.

SUBTONIC, the note situated a semitone below the key note.

SUDDEN MODULATION, that in which the modulating chord is preceded by one which is not doubtful. See *Gradual Modulation*.

SUITE, (*F.*) a series, a collection; as, *une suite de pieces*, a series of lessons.

SUL, (*I.*) on or upon; as, *sul A*, on the A string of the violin, &c.; *sul ponticello*, on or near the bridge.

SUO LOCO, (*L.*) in its own or usual place.

SUONO, (*I.*) a sound.

SUPER, (*L.*) above, over.

SUPERDOMINANT, the note next above the dominant in the scale.

SUPERFLUOUS INTERVALS, augmented intervals.

SUPERIUS, (*L.*) the upper part of any composition.

SUPERSUS, name formerly given to trebles when their station was very high in the scale.

SUPERTONIC, the note above the tonic or key-note.

SUPERTONIQUE, (*F.*) the supertonic, or second note of the scale.

SUPPOSED BASE, lowest note of a chord when not the fundamental one.

SUR, (*F.*) on; as, *sur la quatrième corde*, on the fourth string.

SUSPENSION, the momentary withholding of a note by retaining some notes of the previous chord.

SUSPENDED CADENCE, several modulations being passed through, instead of leading directly from the dominant chord to that of the key-note.

SUSTAINED, notes are said to be sustained when their sound is continued through their whole power or length.

SVEGLIATO, (*I.*) a gay and lively manner of playing or singing.

SWELL, that portion of an organ which consists of a number of pipes enclosed in a box; with this box a pedal communicates, by which it may be gradually opened or shut, and thus the tone made lower by degrees.

SYMPHONY, } the introductory and concluding instrumental
SYMPHONIE, (*F.*) } parts of a song; also, an instrumental composition, consisting of several movements, and designed for a full orchestra.

SYMPHONIOUS, instruments or voices that are in symphony.

SYMPHONIST, one who composes symphonies.

SYMPHONIALE, (*Gk.*) a word prefixed to old canons, or perpetual fugues, to indicate that they are in unison.

SYNAPHE, (*Gk.*) the conjunction of two tetrachords.

SYNAULIA, (*Gk.*) in ancient music, a concert of flute players, who answered each other alternately, without any union of the voice.

SYNCOPATION, forming one continued sound, by connecting an unaccented note with the following accented one, either in the same or in different bars.

SYNCOPATE, SYNCOPATO, (*I.*) syncopated, bound together.

SYNCOPE, (*F.*) a syncopation.

SYNNEMENON, (*Gk.*) the third tetrachord of the ancients.

——————— DIATONOS, (*Gk.*) third chord of the tetrachord.

SYNTONIC, (*Gk.*) a species of the diatonic genus among the

ancients, in which the tetrachord was divided into a semitone and two equal tones.

SYNTONO LYDIAN, one of the ancient modes.

SYRINGA, (*L.*) Pandean pipes, or Pan's pipes.

SYSIGIA, (*Gk.*) a pleasing combination of sounds.

SYSTEMA PERFECTUM, the bis-diapason.

——— TEMPERATO, (*I.*) present system of tones.

——— PARTICIPARTO, a division of the octave or diapason into twelve semitones.

T.

TABLATURA, TABLATURE, (*I.*) the ancient mode of writing music by letters instead of notes.

TABOR, a small drum, generally used to accompany the pipe in dances.

TABRET, a drum of the ancient Hebrews.

TACCI SI, (*I.*) to be silent.

TACE, (*I.*) silent.

TACET, (*L.*) a word which implies that, during a movement or part of a movement, some particular instrument is to be silent; as, *flauto tacet*, the flute is not to play.

TAILLE, (*F.*) the tenor voice or part.

TAIL-PIECE, that piece of wood to which the strings of bow instruments are fastened.

——— TELLERS, name given by the Irish to their bards or harpers.

TAKT, (*G.*) the bar.

TAKTART, (*G.*) the species of time or measure.

TAKTSTRICH, (*G.*) the lines which mark the division of a piece into bars; the bar-line.

TALON, (*F.*) the heel of the bow, that part near the nut.

TAMBOUR, (*F.*) a military or great drum.

——— DE BASQUE, (*F.*) a tambourine.

TAMBOURINE, a well-known pulsatile instrument, like the head of a drum, with jingles placed round it to increase the noise.

TAMBURO, (*I.*) a drum.

TAMBURONE, (*I.*) the great drum.

TAMTAM, an Indian instrument of percussion, like our tambourine.

TANTO, (*I.*) not so much, not too much.

TANTUM ERGO, (*L.*) a hymn sung at the benediction in the Catholic service.

TARANTELLA, (*I.*) a peculiar sort of dance, supposed to have the virtue of curing the bite of a venomous species of spider, called the tarantella.

TARDANDO, (*I.*) See *Ritardando*.

TARDO, (*I.*) slowly, in a dragging manner.

TASTATUR, (*G.*) } the key-board of a piano-forte, &c.
TASTIERA, (*I.*) }

TASTO, (*I.*) the touch of any instrument.

——— SOLO, these words are used in organ and piano-forte music, to indicate that certain bass notes are not to be accompanied by chords in the right hand.

TATTOO, the rapid beat of a drum.

TEDESCA, TEDESCO, (*I.*) in the German style.

TE DEUM, (*L.*) a hymn of thanksgiving.

TELL-TALE, an instrument attached to an organ, which, by rising or falling, indicates the exhaustion of wind.

TEMA, (*I.*) a subject or theme.

TEMPERAMENT, (*F.*) a term used in the mathematical theory of sound, in tuning, &c.

TEMPESTOSO, (*I.*) in a tempestuous manner, violently agitated.

TEMPESTA, a passage in imitation of a storm.

TEMPO, (*I.*) the degree of movement.

——— A, or IN, (*I.*) in time. An expression used after some relaxation in the measure, to indicate a return to the original degree of movement.

——— A PIACERE, the time at pleasure.

——— COMMODO, (*I.*) in a convenient degree of quickness.

——— FRETTOLSO, accelerated time.

——— GIUSTO, (*I.*) in exact or strict time.

——— ORDINARIO, in usual time.

——— PERDUTO, a gradual decrease of time.

——— PRIMO, (*I.*) indicates a return to the original time.

——— RUBATO, (*I.*) implies that the time is to be alternately quickened and retarded, but so that one process may compensate for the other.

——— DI BALLO, (*I.*) in dance time.

———— CAPELLA, in church style.

TEMPO DI GAVOTTA, (*I.*) in gavot time.
———— MARCIA, in time of a march.
———— MENUETTO, (*I.*) in the time of a minuet.
———— POLLACCE, a medium time, between *andante* and *allegro*.
———— VALSE, (*I.*) in the time of a waltz.
TEMPORAGIATO, (*I.*) this word indicates that there is to be a pause, in order to afford the voice or instrument an opportunity of introducing an extemporary grace or embellishment.
TEMPS, TEMS, (*F.*) time; also, the various parts or divisions of the bar.
——— FOIBLE, (*F.*) the weak parts of the bar.
——— FORT, (*F.*) the strong parts of the bar.
——— FRAPPÉ, (*F.*) the accented parts, or down-beats.
——— LÉVÉ, (*F.*) the unaccented parts, or up-beats.
TENDREMENT, (*F.*) affectionately, tenderly.
TENEBRÆ, (*L. Pl.*) the Catholic evening service during holy week.
TENELLA, a burden of ancient Greek songs.
TENERAMENTE, TENEREZZA, *con*, TENERO, (*I.*) tenderly.
TENIR, (*F.*) to hold, as a violin, a bow, &c.
TENOR, the highest male voice.
——— BASE, a man's voice midway between base and tenor.
——— CLEF, the C clef when on the fourth line.
——— VIOLIN, a violin of low tone.
TENORE, (*I.*) the tenor voice or tenor singer; a high male voice.
TENORSCHLÜSSEL, TENORZEICHEN, (*G.*) the tenor clef.
TENSILE, such instruments as have strings are so called.
TENTH, interval embracing an octave and a third.
TENUTE, TENUTO, TEN., *abb.*, (*I.*) implies that a note or notes must be held on, sustained, or kept down the full time.
TEORETICO, (*I.*) a theorist.
TEORIA, (*I.*) theory.
TEPIDAMENTE, TEPIDITA, *con*, (*I.*) with coldness and indifference.
TER, (*I.*) thrice.
—— UNCA, the name formerly given to a demisemiquaver.
TERNARY MEASURE, a three-fold measure.
TERREMOTO, a representation of an earthquake, an example of

which is contained in Haydn's "Last Words of the Savior on the Cross."

TERZ, (*G.*) }
TERZA, (*I.*) } the interval of a third.

TERZETTO, (*I.*) a short trio or piece for three voices or instruments.

TERZINA, (*I.*) a triplet.

TESTO, (*I.*) text or subject of a composition. The word is also applied by the Italians to the poetry of a song.

TESTUDO, name given by the Greeks to the lyre of Mercury.

TETARTOS, (*Gk.*) the four modes of the ancients, called the Mixolydian.

TETRACHORD, a system of four sounds among the ancients, in which the extremes were fixed, but the middle sounds were varied according to the mode.

TETRADIAPASON, the Greek appellation of the quadruple octave.

TETRANONON, Greek name of an interval of four tones.

THEILE, (*G. Pl.*) parts or capital divisions of the bar.

THEME, (*F.*) a subject.

THEORBO, an ancient stringed instrument of the lute kind.

THEORIE, (*F.*) theory.

THEORICIEN, (*F.*) a theorist.

THEORIST, a musician who studies and explains the philosophy of music.

THEURGIC HYMNS, songs of incantation; the first hymns of which we have any account in Greece.

THIRD, an interval of three degrees.

THIRTEENTH, an interval of an octave and a sixth.

THIRTY-SECOND NOTE, a demisemiquaver.

THOROUGH BASS, the art of accompanying a figured bass on the piano or organ.

THRENODIA, (*L.*) a funeral song.

TIBIA, the ancient Roman flute.

TIBIÆ PARES, (*L.*) two flutes played by one person.

TIBICEN, (*L.*) an ancient flute player.

TIES, curved lines drawn over notes.

TIED NOTES, connected notes, or those having a tie above them.

TIERCE, (*F.*) a third. The name of *Tierce* is also given to an organ-stop, which is tuned in the relation of a major third to the principal, or a major tenth above the diapasons.

TIERCE DE PICARDIE. It was formerly the custom to conclude almost every piece written in a minor key with the major common chord of the tonic. This conclusion obtained the name of *Tierce de Picardie,* as the custom was supposed to have originated in that province of France.

TIMBALLES, (*F.*) the kettle drums.

TIMBRE, (*F.*) the degree and quality of vibration and tone peculiar to any instrument.

TIMBREL, an ancient Hebrew instrument, like a tambourine.

TIME TABLE, a representation of the several notes in music, showing their relative lengths or durations.

TIMOROSO, (*I.*) with awe and timidity.

TIMPANI, or TYMPANI, (*I.*) the kettle drums.

TINTINNABULUM, (*L.*) little bells.

TIPPING, placing the end of the tongue on the roof of the mouth, in order to produce certain tones on a flute.

TIRANNA, a Spanish national air.

TIRASSE, (*F.*) the mechanism by which the pedals of an organ act upon the keys, by pulling them down.

TIRATA, (*I.*) a term formerly applied to any number of notes of equal value or length, moving in conjoint degrees.

TIRA TUTTO, (*I.*) a pedal or draw-stop in an organ, which, acting upon all the stops at once, enables the player to obtain the full power of the instrument.

TIRÉ, (*F.*) drawn. This term is used in violin music to denote a down bow.

TOCCATA, (*I.*) a movement of difficult execution for a single instrument, generally the piano-forte.

TOCCATINA, (*I.*) a short toccato.

TON, (*F.*) a tone or interval of a major second. Also the pitch of any note.

TON, (*F.*) the key, as, *le ton d'ut,* the key of C.

TONART, (*G.*) mode.

TONAUSWEICHUNG, (*G.*) modulation.

TONATILLAS, (*S.*) national Spanish airs, sung to a guitar accompaniment.

TONE. This word is received in various senses. First, to signify a certain degree of distance or interval between two sounds, as in the major tone and the minor tone. Secondly, it implies a prop-

12*

erty of sound, by which it comes under the relation of grave and acute.

TONFÜHRUNG, (*G.*) modulation.

TONLÆUM, in ancient music, one of the divisions of the chromatic genus.

TONIC, the key-note is so called by theorists.

TONICA, (*I.*) tonic.

TONIQUE, (*F.*) the tonic or key-note of a piece.

TONKUNST, (*G.*) the science of music.

TONLEITER, (*G.*) the scale.

TONORIUM, (*L.*) a pitch-pipe used by the ancient Romans to regulate the voices of orators, actors, and singers.

TON PATHETIQUE, (*F.*) a plaintive tone.

TONSCHLUSS, (*G.*) a cadence.

TONS DE L'EGLISE, (*F.*) the Church modes or tones.

TONSETZER, (*G.*) a composer.

TONSTÜCK, (*G.*) a musical composition.

TONSTUFE, (*G.*) a degree of the stave.

TONWISSENSCHAFT, (*G.*) the science of music.

TOSTO, (*I.*) swift, or soon.

TOUCHES, (*F.*) the keys of the piano or organ.

TRACHEA, (*L.*) the windpipe.

TRADOTTO, (*I.*) arranged, adapted.

TRAIT, (*F.*) a run, or passage.

TRAITÉ, (*F.*) } a treatise either on the practice or the theory
TRATTATO, (*I.*) } of music.

TRASCINANDO, tardy movements.

TRANQUILLO, TRANQUILLAMENTE, TRANQUILLITA, *con*, TRANQUILLEZZA, *con*, (*I.*) with tranquillity.

TRANSIENT MODULATION, passing modulation; such as quits a key almost as soon as it is entered upon.

——— CHORD, a chord introduced in order to form an harmonious transition between two chords.

TRANSITION, in harmony, changing the genus or mode in a sensible, but regular manner.

TRANSPOSITION, changing a composition into another key from that in which it is written.

TRANSPOSED, removed into another key.

TRAVERSO, (*I.*) } the German flute.
TRAVERSIÈRE, (*F.*) }

TRE, (*I.*) three; as, *à tre*, for three voices or instruments.

TREBLE, the acute part, that which in general contains the melody.

TREMENDO, (*I.*) with a tremendous expression, horribly.

TREMANDO, TREMOLANDO, TREMOLATE, TREMOLO, (*I.*) implies the reiteration of a note or chord with great rapidity, so as to produce a tremulous kind of motion.

TRENISE, (*F.*) one of the twelve movements of the quadrille.

TRIAD, a chord of three notes, a common chord.

TRIADE SEMIDIATONICA, a common chord, comprising two small thirds.

TRIA HARMONICA, (*L.*) a triad, or common chord.

—— **DEFICIENS,** (*L.*) an imperfect triad.

TRIANGLE, a steel instrument of a triangular form.

TRIBACH, a musical foot, composed of three short notes.

TRICINIUM, a composition in three parts.

TRI-DIAPASON, (*Gk.*) a triple octave, or twenty-second.

TRIGON, a three-stringed instrument, resembling the lyre of the ancient Greeks.

TRIGONUM, an ancient instrument of Phrygian invention.

TRIHEMITONE, an interval consisting of three half-tones.

TRILLANDO, (*I.*) a succession of shakes on different notes.

TRILLE, (*F.*)
TRILLER, (*G.*) } a shake.
TRILLO, (*I.*)

TRILLERKETTE, (*G.*) a chain of shakes.

TRILLETTE, (*F.*) a short trill or shake.

TRIMELES, an air in ancient music for the flute.

TRIMETERS, ancient lyrical verses.

TRINKLEID, (*G.*) a bacchanalian or drinking song.

TRIO, (*I.*) a piece for three voices or instruments. This term also denotes a second movement to a waltz, march, minuet, &c., which always leads back to a repetition of the first or principal movement.

TRIOLET, (*F.*) a triplet.

TRIPLE CROCHE, (*F.*) a demisemiquaver.

——— **COUNTERPOINT,** counterpoint in three parts, all of which are invertible.

——— **PROGRESSION,** an expression in old music, implying a series of fifths.

——— **TIMES,** such as have an odd number of parts in a bar.

TRIPLET, a group of three notes arising from the division of a note into three equal parts of the next inferior duration.

TRIPLUM, former name of the treble.

TRIPODIAN, (*Gk.*) an ancient stringed instrument, of difficult performance.

TRISAGION, a hymn in which the word *holy* is repeated three times in succession.

TRITE, a Greek term, signifying three, or third.

TRITONE, } a superfluous or augmented fourth.
TRITONO, (*I.*) }
TRITONUS, (*L.*) }

TRITOS, (*Gk.*) the Æolian modes of the ancients.

TROCHEE, a dissyllabic foot, composed of one long and one short syllable.

TROLL, similar to catch-singing.

TROMBA, (*I.*) a trumpet.

——— **DI BASSO**, (*I.*) the bass trumpet.

——— **MARINA**, (*I.*) the trumpet marine, a species of monochord.

TROMBETTA, (*I.*) a small-sized trumpet.

TROMBONE, (*I.*) a very powerful and rough-toned instrument of the trumpet kind, but much larger, and with a sliding tube.

TROMBONNE, (*F.*) the trombone.

TROMBONO PICCOLO, a small sacbut.

TROMMEL, (*G.*) the great drum.

TROMP DE BEARN, (*F.*) the Jew's harp.

TROMPETTE, (*F.*) the trumpet.

TRONCO, an intimation that the sounds are to be cut short or ended before their natural termination.

TROOP, a quick march.

TROPER, a book formerly used in the Church, containing the chants.

TROPPO, (*I.*) too much. This word is generally preceded by the negative *non*; as, *adagio non troppo*, not too slow.

——— **CARICATA**, (*I.*) is said of an air when overburdened with accompaniments.

TROUBADOURS, the early poet-musicians of Provence.

TRUGSCHLUSS, (*G.*) a deceptive cadence; an unusual and unexpected resolution of a discord.

TUBA, a trumpet.

TUDESCO, in German style. Same as *Tedesco.*

TUNE, a succession of measured sounds.

TUNER, one who rectifies the false sounds of musical instruments.

TUNING-FORK, a steel utensil used for the purpose of tuning instruments, or pitching tunes.

——— HAMMER, a steel or iron utensil used by tuners; with the head of the hammer, the pegs on which the wires are wound are driven into their sockets; and, at the bottom of the handle, a square aperture, which fits the tops of the pegs, enables the tuner to relax or distend the wires.

TUONI ECCLESIASTICI, (*I. Pl.*) the ecclesiastical modes or tones.

TURCA, TURCA ALLA, (*I.*) in the Turkish style.

TURN, an embellishment, consisting of the note on which the turn is made, the note above it, and the semitone below it.

TUTTA, TUTTE, TUTTI, TUTTO, (*I.*) all; as, *con tutta forza,* with all possible force. *Tutti* expresses the entrance of all the instruments before or after a solo.

——— FORZA, (*I.*) with the utmost vehemence, as loud as possible.

TUTTE CORDE, (*I.*) upon all the strings. This term is sometimes met with in music for the piano, to imply that the pedal which shifts the movement must no longer be pressed down.

TUTRICE MUSICA, a female teacher of music.

TWELFTH, an interval of twelve diatonic degrees; an organ-stop tuned a twelfth above the principal.

TYMPANI, (*I.*) the kettle drums.

TYMPANO, or TYMPANUM, a musical instrument of the ancients, similar to a tambourine.

TYROLIENNE, (*F.*) a dance peculiar to the inhabitants of the Tyrol.

U.

UBERMÄSSIGE, (*G.*) augmented, superfluous in regard to intervals.

ÜBUNG, (*G.*) an exercise or study for any musical instrument.

UDITO, (*I.*) the sense of hearing.

UDITORE, (*I.*) an auditor, a hearer.

UGUALE, UGUALMENTE, (*I.*) equally, all alike.

UMANA, (*I.*) human; as, *voce umana*, the human voice.

UMKEHRUNG, (*G.*) inversion, in speaking of chords.

UN, UNA, UNO, (*I.*) a; as, *un poco*, a little.

UNA CORDA, (*I.*) implies that a passage is to be played upon only one string.

UNCA, (*L.*) the old name for a quaver.

UNDULATION, an agitation of the air, or waving movements of the voice.

UNEQUAL VOICES, those compositions in which male and female voices are employed are said to be for unequal voices.

UNESSENTIAL NOTES, those which form no part of the harmony.

UNGERADE TAKTART, (*G.*) triple time.

UNHARMONISCHER QUERSTAND, (*G.*) a false relation.

UNISON, or UNIS, a consonance, or concord of sounds.

UNISONUS, or UNISONANT, a term applied to those sounds which are of the same degree of acuteness or gravity.

UNISONI, (*I. Pl.*) this term implies that two, three, or more parts are to play in unison with each other; or, if this be not practicable, at least in octaves.

UNISONO, (*I.*) a unison.

UNIVOCAL, a term formerly applied to octaves and its replicates.

UNMUSICAL, jarring, dissonant sounds.

UN POCO RITENUTO, gradually slower.

UPIRGE, a song consecrated by the ancient Greeks to Diana.

USUS, a branch of the ancient melopœia, which comprehended the rules for regulating a succession of sounds.

UT, a monosyllable used by the French, to name and solfa the note C.

— QUEANT LAXIS, (*L.*) the commencing words of the hymn to St. John the Baptist, from which hymn Guido is said to have taken the syllables, *ut, re, mi, fa, sol, la,* for his system of solmization.

V.

V is used by the Italians as an abbreviation of the word violin; as, are VV. for violini or violins.

VA, (*I.*) go on; as, *va crescendo*, continue to increase in loudness.

VACCILANDO, wavering, fluctuating.

VAGO, (*I.*) with a vague expression.

VALCE, (*I.*)
VALSE, (*F.*) } a waltz.

VALEUR, (*F.*)
VALUE, } length of notes in respect to time.

VALSE A DEUX TEMS, (*F.*) a modern waltz, in which the dances make two steps in each measure.

VARIATIONS, ornamented repetitions, or various combinations of the same part.

VARIATO, varied, changed, altered.

VARIAMENTO, (*I.*) in a free and varied manner.

VARIAZIONI, (*I.*) variations.

VARIE, (*F.*) varied, arranged with variations.

VAUDEVILLE, (*F.*) a short, interesting dramatic entertainment, interspersed with little airs.

VEEMENTE, VEEMENZA, *con*, (*I.*) vehemently, forcibly.

VELATO, (*I.*) veiled, indistinct.

VELLUTATO, (*I.*) softly and smoothly.

VELOCE, or **CON VELOCITA**, (*I.*) in a rapid time. The term is sometimes used to signify that a particular passage is to be played as quick as possible.

VELOCISSIMO, (*I.*) with extreme rapidity.

VENEZIANA, *alla*, (*I.*) in the Venetian style.

VERÄNDERUNGEN, (*G. Pl.*) variations.

VERBINDUNG, (*G.*) combination.

VERILAY, a rural ballad, a vaudeville.

VERMINDERTE, (*G.*) diminished, in speaking of intervals.

VERSE, a portion of an anthem or service intended to be performed by one singer to each part, and not in chorus like the rest.

——— **ANTHEM**, an anthem containing one or more verses.

——— **SERVICE**, a service in which verses are introduced.

VERSETTE, (*G.*) short movements for the organ, intended as preludes, interludes, or postludes to psalm tunes, &c.

VERSETTO, (*I.*) a short or little verse.

VERSETZEN, (*G.*) to transpose.

VERSETZUNG-ZEICHEN, (*G.*) marks of transposition; the *sharp*, the *flat*, and the *natural*.

VERSI SCIOLTI, (*I.*) blank verse.

VERSO, (*I.*) verse.

——— FESCENNINI, nuptial songs of the people of Fescennia.

VERWANDT, (*G.*) related, relative as to the keys.

VERWECHSLUNG, (*G.*) a change or mutation.

VERZIERUNG, (*G.*) embellishment, variation.

VESPERÆ, (*L.*) vespers or evening service in the Catholic church.

VESPERS, the evening service in the Catholic church.

VESPERTINI PSALMI, (*I.*) evening hymns.

VIBRANTE, (*I.*) a peculiar manner of touching the keys of the piano.

VIBRATISSIMO, (*I.*) the superlative of *vibrato.*

VIBRATE, VIBRATO, (*I.*) with a strong, vibrating quality of tone.

VIDO, (*I.*) } VUIDE, (*F.*) } terms used in music for such stringed instruments as the violin, violoncello, &c., to signify that a particular note must be played on the open string.

VIELLE, (*F.*) the hurdy-gurdy.

VIETATO, prohibited.

VIERTELNOTE, (*G.*) a crotchet.

VIGOROSO, VIGOROSAMENTE, (*I.*) boldly, vigorously.

VILLANELLA, VILANELLE, (*I.*) the name of an old rustic dance.

VIOLA, (*I.*) the tenor.

VIOLARS, strolling violinists of the twelfth century.

VIOL D'AMORE, (*I.*) } VIOLE D'AMOUR, (*F.*) } an instrument with six strings, resembling the violin in form, but with frets.

VIOL DE BRACCIA, (*I.*) the alto viola, or counter-tenor violin, so called because held on the arm or shoulder.

——— DA GAMBA, a stringed instrument so called; during the performance, it is held between the legs.

VIOLENTIMENTE, VIOLENZA, *con*, (*I.*) with violence.

VIOLETTA, small alto-viol.

——— MARINA, a stringed instrument, introduced in England in 1732.

VIOLIN, a well-known stringed instrument, of brilliant tone and active execution.

——— SCHLÜSSEL, VIOLINZEICHEN, (*G.*) the treble clef, used for the violin, flute, &c.

VIOLINIST, a performer on the violin.

VIOLINO, (*I.*) the violin.
——— PRINCIPALE, (*I.*) the principal violin part.
VIOLON, (*F.*) the violin.
VIOLONCELLE, (*F.*) } the bass violin.
VIOLONCELLO, (*I.*) }
VIOLONO, (*I.*) the double bass.
VIRGINAL, an old keyed instrument, in high favor with Queen Elizabeth and the ladies of her time.
VIRGULA, one of the ten notes of the middle ages.
VIRGULUM, former name of the branch of a note.
VIRTUOSO, (*I.*) a musician who greatly excels on any particular instrument.
VIRTU, VIRTUOSITA, manliness, or taste and address in performance.
VISTAMENTE, (*I.*) }
VITE, (*F.*) } with quickness.
VITEMENT, (*F.*) }
VIVACE, VIVACEMENTE, quick and lively.
VIVAMENTE, or CON VIVACITA, (*I.*) with briskness and animation.
VIVACISSIMO, (*I.*) with extreme vivacity.
VIVACITA, (*I.*) vivacity; as, *con vivacita*, vivaciously.
VIVENTE, VIVEZZA, *con*, VIVO, (*I.*) animated, lively.
VOCAL, music composed for the voice.
VOCALIZE, to practise singing on the vowels, chiefly the Italian A.
VOCALIZZI, (*I.*) vocal exercises to be sung on the vowels.
VOCE, (*I.*) the voice.
——— MUSICALE, (*I.*) by this term, the Italians distinguished the tonic or major key-note.
——— SOLA, (*I.*) to be sung without an accompaniment.
——— DI CAMERA, (*I.*) a voice suited for private rather than for public singing.
——— PETTO, (*I.*) the chest or natural voice.
——— TESTA, (*I.*) the head voice; that is, the falsetto or feigned voice.
VOICE, sound or sounds produced by the vocal organs in singing.
VOIX ARGENTINE, (*F.*) a clear, fine-toned voice.
——— MONOTONE, a monotonous voice.
VOLANTE, (*I.*) in a light and rapid manner.

VOLATA, VOLATINA, (*I.*)
VOLATE, VOLATINE, (*F.*) } a rapid succession of notes.

VOLKSLIED, (*G.*) a national song.

VOLL, (*G.*) full; as, *mit volle Orgel*, full organ.

VOLLKOMMEN, (*G.*) perfect.

VOLONTÉ, (*F.*) will, pleasure; as, *à volonté*, at will.

VOLTA, (*I.*) time of playing a movement; as, *prima volta*, the first time of playing; *seconda volta*, the second time, &c.

VOLTARE, or VOLTI, turn over, or change.

VOLTE, (*I.*) an obsolete dance resembling the Galliard, written in $\frac{3}{4}$ time.

VOLTI SUBITO, (*I.*) turn over the page quickly.

VOLUBILITA, *con*, VOLUBILMENTE, (*I.*) with volubility and freedom of performance.

VOLUME, the compass of a voice.

VOLUNTARY, a piece for the organ, generally consisting of two or three movements, calculated to display the capabilities of the instrument and the skill of the player.

VON, (*G.*) by; often occurs in German titles.

VORAUSNAHME, (*G.*) an anticipation in melody or harmony.

VORBEREITUNG, (*G.*) a preparation.

VORHALT, (*G.*) a suspension or retardation either in melody or harmony.

VORSCHLAG, (*G.*) an *appoggiatura*.

VORSPIELE, (*G.*) an introductory movement; a prelude in organ playing.

VORZEICHNUNG, (*G.*) the signature.

VOX, (*L.*) voice.

—— ACUTA, (*L.*) an acute or high voice.

—— GRAVIS, (*L.*) a grave or low voice.

VUIDE, (*F.*) open; as, *corde vuide*, in violin music, indicates the open string.

W.

WALTZ, a dance originating in Germany, the music of which is usually in $\frac{3}{8}$ measure.

WALZER, (*G.*) a waltz.

WARBLE, in a manner imitative of the songs of birds.

WAYGHTES, WAITS, persons who, about Christmas, play psalm tunes, &c., in the streets during the night.

WECHSELNOTEN, (*G. Pl.*) irregular transient notes; appoggiaturas.
WEICHE, (*G.*) minor in respect to keys and mode.
WEITE HARMONIE, (*G.*) dispersed harmony.
WELSH HARP, an instrument having about one hundred strings.
WESENTLICH, (*G.*) essential.
WHOLE NOTE, a semibreve.
WIEDERHOLUNG, (*G.*) repetition.
WINDLADE, (*G.*) the wind-chest of an organ.
WIND INSTRUMENTS, those instruments, the sounds of which are produced by the breath, or by the wind of bellows.
WIRBEL, (*G.*) a peg of a violin, tenor, &c.
WRIST GUIDE, that part of Logier's Chisplast which guides the wrist.

Z.

ZAMPOGNO, (*I.*) in the style of the bagpipe.
ZARGE, (*G.*) the sides of any musical instrument.
ZEITMASS, (*G.*) the time or degree of movement.
ZELO, *con*, ZELOSAMENTE, ZELOSO, (*I.*) with seal; enthusiastically.
ZERSTREUT, (*G.*) dispersed.
ZINGARESA, *alla*, (*I.*) in the gypsy style.
ZINKE, (*G.*) a kind of rustic pipe, no longer used; a cornet.
ZITHER, (*G.*) the guitar.
ZOPPO, (*I.*) in a limping manner. A style of melody in which a long note is always placed between two short notes.
ZUFÄLLIG, (*G.*) accidental.
ZUFFOLO, (*I.*) a little flute or flageolet, chiefly used to teach birds to sing.
ZURÜCKHALTUNG, (*G.*) retardation.
ZUSAMMENGESETZT, (*G.*) compound, in speaking of times.
ZWISCHENSPEIL, (*G.*) an interlude in organ playing.
ZWISCHENRÄUME, (*G.*) the spaces between the lines of the stave.
ZWEISTIMMIG, (*G.*) for two voices or parts.
ZWEYFACHE INTERVALLEN, (*G. Pl.*) compound intervals.
ZWEYKLANG, (*G.*) a chord of two sounds.

ABBREVIATIONS.

Accel. . . . . Accellerando
Acc. . . . } Accompagnamento
Accom. . }
Ad lib. . . . Ad libitum
Ad^{o}. . . . . . Adagio
Affet^{o}. . . . . Affetuoso
Affret^{o}. . . . Affrettando
All^{o}. . . . . . Allegro
All^{tto}. . . . . Allegretto
All 8va. . . . All' ottava
Al Seg. . . . Al Segno
And^{no}. . . . Andantino
And^{te}. . . . Andante
Arp^{o}. . . . . Arpeggio
A temp. . . A tempo

B. C. . . . . Basso Continuo
Brill. . . . . Brillante

Cal^{o}. . . . . . Calando
C.B. . . . . . Contrabasso
Cello. . . . . Violoncello
Clar. . . . . Clarinet
Col C . . . Col Canto
Co 1mo. . . . Canto Primo
Con Esp. . Con Espressione
Cres. . . . . Crescendo
C^{to}. . . . . . Concerto

D. C. . . . . Da Capo
Decres. . . . Decrescendo
Diap. . . . . Diapason
Dim. . . . . Diminuendo
Dol. . . . . . Dolce
Dolciss. . . Dolcissimo
D. S. . . . . Dol Segro

Energ^{e}. . . . Energicamente
Espress. . . Espressivo

F. . . . . . . Forte
Fag. . . . . . Fagotto

FF. . . . . . Fortissimo
FFF. . . . . Very fortissimo
Fl. . . . . . . Flauto or Flauti
Fz. . . . . . . Forzando
Fp. . . . . . . Forte, and then Piano; when applied to a single note, it marks a strong accent.

Grand^{o}. . . Grandioso
Graz^{o}. . . . Grazioso

Introd. . . . Introduzione

Leg. . . . . . Legato
Leggier. . . Leggiero
L. H. . . . . Left hand

Maest^{o}. . . . Maestoso
Man^{do}. . . . Mancando
Magg. . . . . Maggiore
M. D. . . . . Mano dritta
M. F. . . . . Mezzo forte
M. M. . . . . Maelzel's Metronome
M. P. . . . . Mezzo piano
M. S. . . . . Mano sinistra
Men. . . . . Meno
Min. . . . . . Minore
Mod^{o}. . . . . Moderato
Mus. Bac. . Bachelor of Music
Mus. Doc. . Doctor of Music
M. V. . . . . Mezza voce

Ob. . . . . . Oboe
Op. . . . . . Opera
Org^{o}. . . . . Organo
8^{a}. or 8va. . Ottava
8va alta. . . Ottava alta, an octave higher
8va bassa. . Ottava bassa, an octave lower
Con 8va. . . Con ottava, with octaves

P.	Piano
Ped.	Pedal
Perden.	Perdendosi
PF.	Piano and then forte
Pizz.	Pizzicato
PP.	Pianissimo
1ma.	Prima
1mo.	Primo
PPP.	Very pianissimo
$Prest^{mo}$.	Prestissimo
Raddol.	Raddolcendo
Rallen. / $Rall^{o}$.	Rallentando
Recit.	Recitativo
R. H.	Right hand
Rf. / Rfz. / Rinf.	Rinforzando
Ritard.	Ritardando
Riten.	Ritenuto
Scherz.	Scherzando
Seg.	Segno
Sem.	Sempre
Sf.	Sforzando
Smorz.	Smorzando
Sost. / Sosten.	Sostenuto
Sym.	Symphony
2da.	Seconda
2do.	Secondo
Stacc.	Staccato
T. S.	Tasto Solo
Tem.	Tempo
Ten.	Tenuto
Tr.	Trillo
Unis.	Unisoni
Var.	Variation
V^{a}.	Viola
V^{o}.	Violino
V^{llo}.	Violoncello
V. S.	Volti subito
V. V.	Violini

PHRASES WHICH OCCUR IN MODERN AUTHORS.

Andante ma non troppo e con tristezza. Not too slow, but with pathos.

Andantino sostenute e semplicemente, il canto un poco più forte. In a sustained and simple style, with the melody somewhat louder than the other notes.

Colla più gran forza e prestezza. As loud and as quick as possible.

Come 'l primo tempo. In the same degree of movement as at first.

Come tempo del tema. Same degree of movement as the theme.

Cantabile, ornamenti ad libitum, ma più tosto pochi e buoni. In a singing style, with embellishments at will, but few and well chosen.

Con abbandono ed espressione. With self-abandon and expression.

Con brio ed animato. Animated and brilliant.

Con 8va ad libitum. With octaves at pleasure.

Crescendo ed incalcando poco a poco. Greatly augmenting the power and increasing the time.

Crescendo poco a poco. Increasing the sound by degrees.

Crescendo e poi diminuendo. Increasing and then diminishing the sound.

Da capo senza repetizione e poi la coda. Begin again, but without any repetition of the strain, and then proceed to the coda.
Dolce con gusto. Sweetly and tastefully.
Dolce e lusingando. In a delicate and insinuating style.
Dolce e piacevolmente espressivo. Soft and with pleasing expression.
Dolce ma marcato. Delicately, but still sufficiently marked.
FF. principalmente il basso. Very loud, especially the bass.
Il terzo dite a tutte le notte di basso. The third finger on all the notes in the bass.
Istesso valore, ma un poco più lento. The same duration, but rather slower.
L'istesso tempo poi a poi di nuovo vivente. The same time, with gradually increasing animation.
Moderato assai con molto sentimento. A very moderate degree of movement, with much feeling.
Piano, sempre staccato e marcato il basso. Soft, with the bass always well marked and detached.
Poco a poco, più di fuoco. With gradually increasing animation and fire.
Poco a poco crescendo, decrescendo. Louder, softer, by degrees.
Poi a poi tutte le corde. All the strings, one after another. An expression used in playing the grand piano-forte.
Segue subito senza cambiare il tempo. Proceed directly and without changing the time.
Segue senza interruzione. Go on without stopping.
Sempre piano e ritenuto. Always more and more soft, and falling off in the degree of movement.
Sempre più decrescendo e più rallentando. Gradually softer and slower.
Sempre più forte . . . . . all ff^mo^. Louder and louder to the fortissimo.
Seconda volta molto crescendo. Much louder the second time of playing.
Sin' al fine. To the end.
Tenete sino alla fine del suono. Keep down the keys as long as the sound lasts.

CHARACTERS USED IN MUSIC.

§ 1. *Names of the Notes.*

In England, and in Germany, the notes are named after the seven letters, A, B, C, D, E, F, G.

The only difference is, that the Germans apply the letter *B* to B flat only, and call our B natural, *H*.

In Italy and France the notes are named la, si, do, re, mi, fa, sol, corresponding to our A, B, C, D, E, F, G.

These notes may be natural, sharp, or flat, and occasionally even double sharp, or double flat.

Thus we have C natural, C sharp, C flat, and, at times, C double sharp, and C double flat.

In France and Italy these notes would respectively be called *do naturelle, do dieze, do bemol, do double dieze, do double bemol*, &c.

The Germans add to the letter which is used to denominate the note in its natural state, *is*, when it is to be made *sharp*, and *es*, when *flat*. Thus, with them,

C sharp	is called	cis,
C flat	———	ces,
C double sharp	———	ciscis,
C double flat	———	cesces.

The stave on which the notes are written.

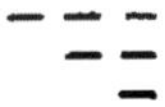

Ledger lines, drawn above or below the stave, to supply additional places for the notes.

Clefs.

Treble or G clef.

C clef, which admits of four situations.

F or bass clef.

§ 2. *Characters relating to the Duration of the Notes, Rests, Dot, &c.*

Breve. Semibreve. Minim. Crotchet.

Quaver. Semiquaver. Demisemiquaver.

&c.

All the above notes may have one, two, or even three *dots* placed after them, to protract their duration.

Each note has a corresponding *rest;* as,

Breve rest, or two bars in any time. Semibreve rest, or generally a single bar rest. Minim rest.

Crotchet rest. Quaver rest. Semiquaver rest. Demisemiquaver rest.

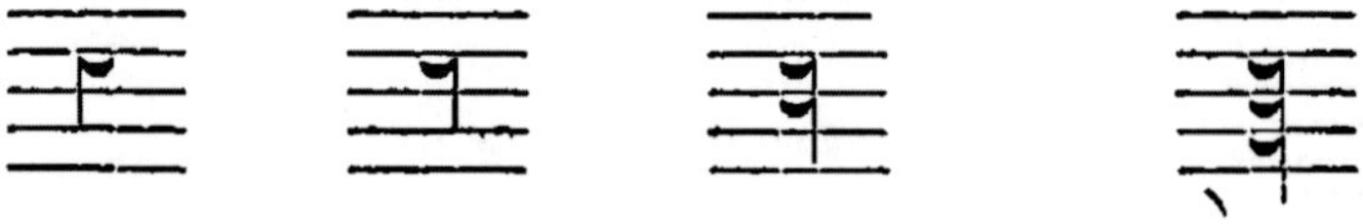

&c.

Rests may be dotted, or doubly or triply dotted, like the notes which they represent.

Notes are sometimes divided into 3, 5, 7, 9, &c., equal parts, instead of 2, 4, or 8, as usual; in this case, the number of parts is expressed by a figure, and a curved line is drawn over it, thus: $\overset{\frown}{3}$, $\overset{\frown}{5}$, $\overset{\frown}{7}$, $\overset{\frown}{9}$, &c.

§ 3. *Marks of Transposition or Alteration of the Pitch of the Natural Notes.*

♯	The sharp.	×	The double sharp.
♭	The flat.	♭♭	The double flat.
♮	The natural.	♮♯	Single sharp after a double sharp.
		♮♭	Single flat after a double flat.

§ 4. *Table of Characters denoting the different Species of Time.*

| | | Bar lines, dividing a movement into small equal portions of duration.

C or ₵ Indicates two minims or four crotchets in each bar.

$\frac{2}{4}$ Indicates two crotchets in each bar.

$\frac{3}{2}$ —— three minims ——

$\frac{3}{4}$ —— three crotchets ——

$\frac{3}{8}$ Indicates three quavers in each bar.

$\frac{6}{4}$ —— six crotchets ——

$\frac{6}{8}$ —— six quavers ——

$\frac{12}{8}$ —— twelve quavers ——

$\frac{12}{16}$ —— twelve semiquavers ——

$\frac{9}{4}$ —— nine crotchets ——

$\frac{9}{8}$ —— nine quavers ——

$\frac{9}{16}$ —— nine semiquavers ——

§ 5. *Other Characters affecting the Duration of the Notes.*

⌒ A *bind* or *tie*, which connects two or more notes of the same name into one longer note.

𝄐 A *pause*, which lengthens at will the duration of a note or rest.

§ 6. *Characters indicating the various Degrees of Loud and Soft.*

< Indicates a *crescendo*, or gradual increase of tone.

> Indicates a *decrescendo*, or gradual decrease.

<> Indicates first a *crescendo*, and then a *decrescendo*.

>< Indicates first a *decrescendo*, and then a *crescendo*.

§ 7. *Marks of Accent and Expression.*

> V Λ ÷ ·̄· } Indicate a stress or marked accent on any single note or chord. The abbreviations *rf*, *sf*, *fz*, *rfz*, *sfz*, *fp*, or even *f* over a single note, are also used for the same purpose.

' ' ' ' Dashes indicate notes struck very short, or staccato; that is, not held their full value.

. . . . Dots, notes struck short, but not in so marked a way as the preceding.

Curve and dots. Notes still less staccato. This is called the *mezzo staccato*.

Slur, or legato mark.

§ 8. *Graces.*

or Indicates the appoggiatura, where superior or inferior.

~ Turn.

Inverted turn.

♭ Turn with the note above made flat.

♯ Turn with the note below made sharp.

tr or tr~~~~~ A shake.

or The vibration or close shake.

(or Indicates that the chord before which it is placed must be sprinkled or arpeggioed.

§ 9. *Characters used to separate a Movement into its component Parts or Strains, Marks of Repetition, &c.*

Double bar.

Double bar, with a repetition of the preceding strain.

Double bar, with a repetition of the following strain.

Double bar, with a repetition of the strain on each side.

Indicates the strain which is to conclude the piece.

§ 10. *Marks of Punctuation, or Rhythm.*

Indicates a *phrase* or incomplete musical idea.

Indicates a *section*, or complete but not independent idea.

O Indicates a *period*, or complete and independent musical sentence.

The ordinary marks of punctuation , ; : . are employed by some composers for a similar purpose.

§ 11. *Miscellaneous Characters.*

{ A *brace*, used to connect two or more staves together in piano-forte, harp, and organ music, or in scores.

= 120 } = 80 } Mark the application of Maelzel's Metronome, &c.

Ped. } Are met with in piano-forte music, to indicate the use of the pedals.

The direct; it is placed upon the same line or space as the note which begins the next line.

} Are often met with in violin music, the former to indicate a *down*, and the latter an *up*, bow.

§ 12. *Marks of Abbreviations.*

Indicates that the long note must be repeated as often as it contains quavers or semiquavers.

 is equivalent to 

 to 

 is equivalent to 

 to 

and

 is equivalent to 

A

SHORT TREATISE

ON

PLAYING THE ORGAN OR PIANO-FORTE

BY FIGURES,

AS USED IN WRITING PSALM TUNES AND OTHER CHURCH MUSIC, WHICH IS COMMON IN THIS COUNTRY.

LESSON I.

COMMON CHORD.

In playing church music, the pupil should look to the two extreme parts, viz. the Base and Soprano, and the figures which are usually written underneath the Base. The other two parts are termed the intermediate parts, (Alto and Tenor) from the fact that they are seldom played below the Base or above the Soprano.

All four parts are played, and sometimes other notes are added to fill up the harmony. The Base is usually played with the left hand, and the Tenor, Alto and So prano with the right, the two intermediate parts being frequently played an octave above where written.

Any letter with its third, fifth, and usually eighth, is termed a common chord, and it is generally played in three different positions, thus:

although there are three other positions, as has been shown in Lesson III on Musical Composition; but as the common chord of any letter is not usually figured, it would be difficult to tell which position it should be played in, without looking to the intermediate parts, if the last three inversions were played.*

Perhaps it would be well for us here to remark, that all the letters bear the same relationship to C, whether high or low, so far as the figuring is concerned; for examples and illustrations see Lesson III.

Sometimes the common chord is figured; when this is the case, it is usually done to contradict some preceding chord. The figures which are used are $\begin{smallmatrix}8\\5\\3\end{smallmatrix}$ either of which singly or together, represent the common chord and positions.

Exercise for the pupil to fill out as it should be played; also, name the different positions, &c.

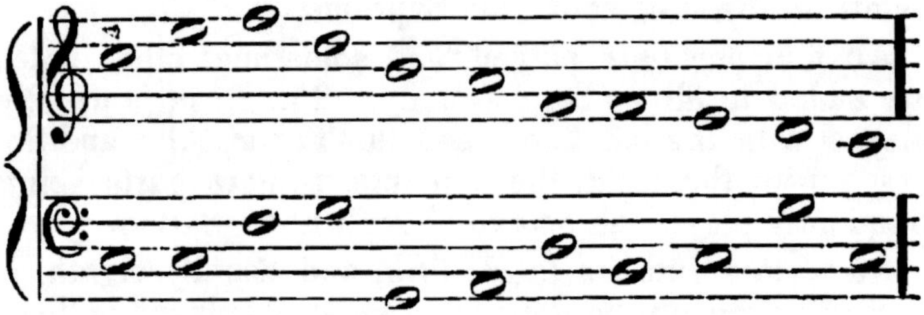

* It is to be regretted that the habit of playing by figures is so much in vogue in this country, as many of the chords must necessarily be played rather imperfect, which would not be the case, if the intermediate parts were brought on the two staffs with the Base and Soprano.

The pupil should now commence playing simple psalm tunes, leaving out the chords which he does not understand, and confining himself to the common chord. He should also be required to name the different positions of each letter which he plays in the Base.

LESSON II.

INVERSIONS OF THE COMMON CHORD.

EVERY common chord is susceptible of two inversions, and to each of the inversions the three different positions may be played, thus.

As the pupil will perceive, the figure to the first inversion is 6—to the second, $^6_4$. When the figure 6 is written under a chord, we refer back a third and play the common chord, to that letter which is a third below the Base, and this is termed the fundamental base of the chord. In the second inversion, we refer back a fifth and play the common chord to the fifth below.

Remark.—It is hoped that the pupil will not put a wrong construction on what has been said respecting the inversion of the common chord. It is not expected that the fundamental base will be played with the left hand, but the real base which is written; yet still preserving the common chord to the fundamental, viz $\begin{smallmatrix}8\\5\\3\end{smallmatrix}$. (See Lesson III on the Elements of Musical Composition.)

Example for the pupil to fill out and play.

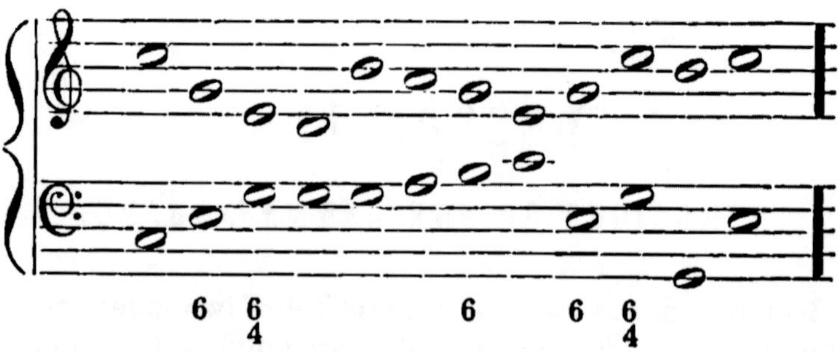

The pupil may now play the same tunes in which he has been practising the common chord, and play the chords of the 6 and $\begin{smallmatrix}6\\4\end{smallmatrix}$ wherever they occur, naming the inversion and position, &c.

LESSON III

CHORD OF THE SEVENTH.

The common chord of any letter with the seventh added, counted up from the base, constitutes the chord of the seventh; three positions are usually played, thus:

Exercise for the pupil to fill out and play.

Practice tunes, and play the chord of the seventh wherever it occurs, naming the position, &c.

The chord of the seventh has three inversions, and to each inversion three positions, thus:

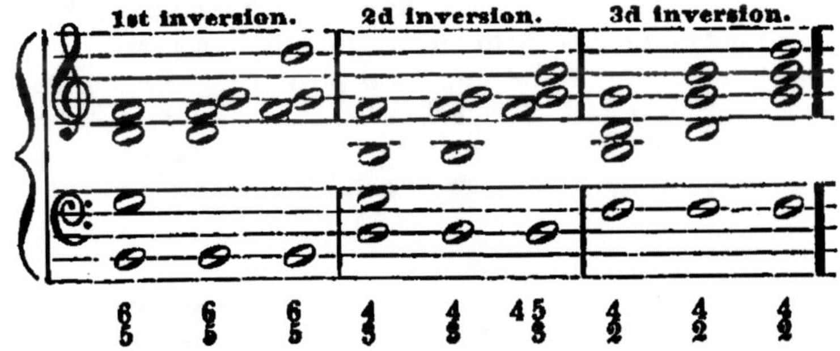

Exercise for the pupil to fill out and play, naming the inversion, position, &c.

Practice tunes, and play the inversions of the seventh wherever they occur, naming the inversion, position, &c.

LESSON IV.

MISCELLANEOUS CHORDS.

THERE are several other chords besides the above, but it will not be necessary to go so minutely into particulars respecting them, if the pupil will only bear in mind the fact, that they are always figured from the real base. Here are most of the remaining chords which are used in common psalm tunes, written out, thus:

* A Sharp, Flat or Natural placed under a chord or figure, always has reference to the third from the real base.

There may be a few other combinations of figures used occasionally, but the above are the principal. If other figures do occur, all the pupil will have to do is to count up from the base; and if he then will not be enabled to play the chord right, he had better look to the intermediate parts, when he will be sure to get the right notes. The pupil should seldom double the third of a chord, as it often leads to bad progressions, &c.

---

* A Sharp, Flat or Natural placed before a figure has the same effect as though placed before a note.

† Two parallels thus, = signify the chord should be continued.

CONCERT MUSIC.

This is the field which presents the greatest scope of development in the treatment of individual instruments, as well as the whole of them conjointly.

The *Symphony* is the highest climax of instrumental music—a combination of several instruments, in which every one appears in more or less rivalship with the other, to participate in the general co-operation for melody and harmony. A brilliant, animated, rich style, grand and vigorous melodies in well-poised alternation with soft and tender thoughts, striking and decisive bases, energetic modulations, the boldest interlacements and imitations of melodies and rhythms, the utmost successive changes, and the most varied union of the instruments, co-operating in the general effect, at one time individually, at another simultaneously—now as principals, now as accompaniment, or reinforcing and filling up the score—such are the characteristic features of the symphony. In order to satisfy these requisites, great mastery of harmony, and knowledge of all the instruments, will be found to be indispensable.

In the *Overture*, the requisites pointed out for the symphony are called for in a less degree. In cases, moreover, where the overture serves as introduction to a work of greater extent, such as an opera, oratorio, &c. its nature and character is defined by the contents of the work itself; inasmuch as its object ought to be to indicate the contents of the composition which it ushers in. The symphony, on the contrary, is an independent, entirely unfettered creation of musical imagination.

The *Concerto* is destined to display the *character* and *capabilities* of an *instrument*, supported and accompanied by the rest of the orchestra, all the instruments of which, however, are not requisite in such co-operation. It is therefore, essential and natural that the instrument in question should act a prominent part, whether it be by means of impressive delivery or mechanical skill. That, on such an occasion, the character of the instrument should be carefully attended to, and its mechanical treatment fully understood by the composer, is a matter of course. A composer and virtuoso, whose aim is a mere accumulation of mechanical intricacies, and who affords no opportunity of gratifying the *feelings* of his hearers by genuine touches of *expression*, does not come within the pale of the foregoing definition; and much less so, if he conceives the *non plus ultra* of "virtuosity" to consist in striving to render things possible which militate against the nature of the instrument. Feats of this kind are pretty much of a piece with those of a rope-dancer, &c.

CHURCH MUSIC.

The object of church music is to assist in the worship of the Almighty, to fill the mind of the hearer with religious feelings, and to raise his thoughts above all earthly considerations. This can only be effected if the *melody* is simple and of a noble character, scorns all unnecessary, tinselly ornaments, and refrains from everything which merely enables the singers or players to exhibit their mechanical dexterity.

It is here that the powers of *harmony* should be rendered available in their greatest energy, without, however, indulging in artificial modulations, or injuring the purity and clearness of the melody by combinations of too complex a nature, and an accumulation of dissonances without object; for that which is truly great must present itself to the mind in the simplest and clearest form.

Church music occurs in a two-fold form, viz., as *choral music* and as *figurate music*.

In choral-chant, the melody moves in the most simple and easy intervals of tone, without any passing notes which might serve the purpose of ornament, in steps at once slow and solemn, and mostly of equal duration.

As the choral melody is to be sung by the whole congregation,* the extent of its range ought not to be great; but limited, if possible, within the space of an octave. Care is also to be taken that the air does not ascend too high or drop too low, in order to render its execution practicable to an assembly composed of voices of so different a pitch. The limits we should be inclined to propose, would be $\bar{d}$ or $\bar{c}$ for the lowest, and $\bar{\bar{e}}$, or at the utmost $\bar{\bar{f}}$, for the highest notes.

Let the harmonic accompaniment, in sacred tunes of several vocal parts as well as for the organ, be simple, noble and energetic, and in accordance with the character of the poetry. It ought neither to be showy and inclining to parade, lest it turn off the attention from the melody, nor too meagre of interest. Do not seek to surprise the hearer by too frequent a use of dissonances, unusual turns, modulations, and transitions; but be careful, at the same time, not to convert simplicity into monotony, by employing, exclusively, fundamental chords and their first inversions.

It is in *figurate music*, where the congregation does not co-operate, that the *chorus* is of primary importance; and here the composer finds ample scope for displaying the powers and capabilities of harmony in their full extent. It is here that an elaborate harmonic development, such as the fugue displays in the highest perfection, will be in its right place, and may be resorted to with the greatest success. But to produce a work of this description, in which, instead of artificial contrivance constituting its only merit, the inspiration of genius shall, throughout, predominate over the highest efforts of mere art, is the greatest

* This is not the case in this country, yet still the remarks will apply to our choirs generally.

problem in musical composition; a problem which, successfully solved, presents the highest masterpiece of which the art is capable.

The vocal solo, which, if ably applied, forms a happy contrast with the energies of the chorus, should not aim at displaying the mechanical dexterity of the singer, which ought to be considered as merely the means of attaining the end proposed. It should breathe the language of that genuine pious feeling which is a stranger to all outward show, and seeks to appear before the Eternal Being in submissive humility. Hence we cannot but condemn, as contrary to the object in view, the arias in several cantatas of no very remote date, in which tasteless and unmeaning divisions, roulades, and other fringe-work distract the attention, and tear and distend the words of the text in the clumsiest manner.

If the student is desirous of practically knowing how the genuine vocal solo for the church ought to be constituted, let him consult some of the arias in Handel's *Messiah*—above all, the admirable soprano song, "I know that my Redeemer liveth;" also the solos in Mozart's *Requiem*, several solos in the masses of Haydn, and in his oratorio, the *Creation.*

Figurate music, with *instrumental accompaniments*, ought only to be resorted to on extraordinary and solemn festivals; while pure vocal music, in combination with the organ, should alone be employed on common occasions. It would also be highly desirable that, in the Protestant Church, music were brought into more intimate union with the divine service, and that the hymns of the congregation were more frequently relieved by choir singing, for it cannot be denied that, in the Catholic Church, music, when it is employed, appears as an essential and integral part of the service, and thus produces a much greater impression than is the case in Protestant communities, into which it is rather admitted by sufferance, and where it stands as it were an insulated stranger. At the same time, we are willing to admit that many of the modern compositions for the Catholic Church are exceedingly frivolous, and far from corresponding with the dignity of genuine church music.

CONTENTS.